THE GREATEST 2019 BOOK OF POLITICAL CARTOONS ON ISSUES OF THE DONALD J. TRUMP PRESIDENCY... Edition I: January–June

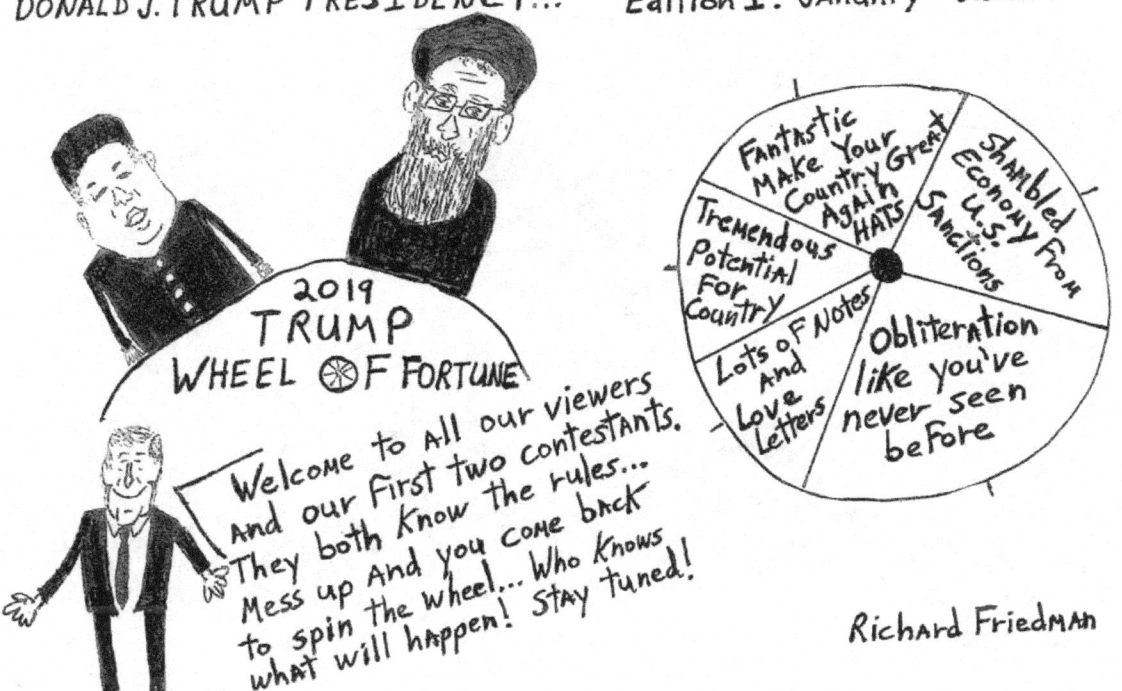

2019
TRUMP
WHEEL OF FORTUNE

Welcome to all our viewers
and our first two contestants.
They both know the rules...
Mess up and you come back
to spin the wheel... Who knows
what will happen! Stay tuned!

Fantastic
Make Your
Country Great
Again HATS

Shambled
Economy From
U.S.
Sanctions

Tremendous
Potential
For
Country

Lots of Notes
And
Love
Letters

Obliteration
like you've
never seen
before

Richard Friedman

Senate Republicans Gently Push Back On Trump's Threatened Tariffs On Mexico... With A Threat to Override President's Veto... Below Senators Mitch McConnell & Chuck Grassley Try Their Luck With A TRUMP STATUE...

I hope you will not go through with your latest Mexican Tariffs!

I do not support your TARIFF threat on Mexico!

CONTENTS
Introduction I

INTRODUCTION I

"The dogmas of the quiet past, are inadequate to the stormy present. The occasion is piled high with difficulty, and we must rise -- with the occasion. As our case is new, we must think anew and act anew. We must disenthrall ourselves, and then we shall save our country."

The above quote is from President Abraham Lincoln's message to Congress on December 1, 1862. This was during the American Civil War, which had been waging since April 12, 1861.

In 2019 if Mr. Robert Mueller finds evidence of criminal conduct involving President Trump. It will be legally arguable as to whether a sitting President can be indicted. The Constitution offers no solution. Lawmakers, pundits, legal analysts and President Trump's Attorney Rudolph W. Giuliani have offered different views. Giuliani has stated the President does not have to comply with a subpoena because he is "the President of the United States."

Whether or not Lincoln's above quote is relevant to this possible 2019 quagmire, is thematic to this author's second book of political cartoons on the Trump Presidency. And what again impelled me to create it.

Richard Friedman

Chapter I
Jan.- March 2019

Trump Starts OFF The Year With Bizarre Cabinet Meeting Saying Mattis Did A Bad Job As Defense Chief
Citing Afghanistan Saying He Would Make A "Good General"   Jan. 3, 2019

We have an area that I brought up with our generals. Where Taliban is here ISIS is here and they're fighting each other. I said why don't you let them fight! Why are we gettin in the middle of it? I said let them fight. They're both our enemies. Let them fight - Then it's: Sir we want to do it... And they end up fighting both of them. I think I would have been a good general...

General Trump In Afghanistan

A Taliban or ISIS defeat is better than fighting two enemies. We just do A deal with the WINNER!

All U.S. Forces STAND DOWN

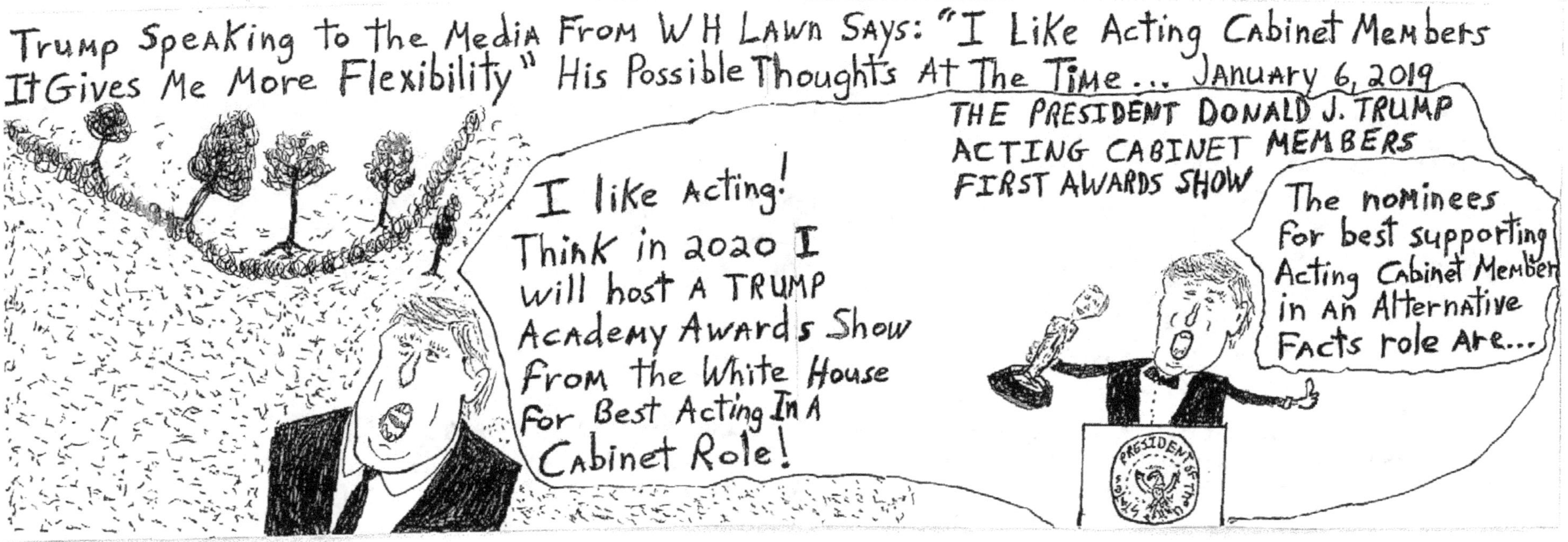
Trump Speaking to the Media From W H Lawn Says: "I Like Acting Cabinet Members It Gives Me More Flexibility" His Possible Thoughts At The Time... January 6, 2019
I like Acting! Think in 2020 I will host A TRUMP Academy Awards Show From the White House For Best Acting In A Cabinet Role!
THE PRESIDENT DONALD J. TRUMP ACTING CABINET MEMBERS FIRST AWARDS SHOW
The nominees for best supporting Acting Cabinet Member in An Alternative Facts role Are...
PRESIDENT OF THE UNITED STATES

Trump Gets A Possible Suggestion For His "Beautiful Wall" From A Well Known Late Night Talk Show Host. This in the Wake of President Stating He Will Be Contacting U.S. Steel Companies For Proposals to Design A "Beautiful Steel Product" January 7, 2019

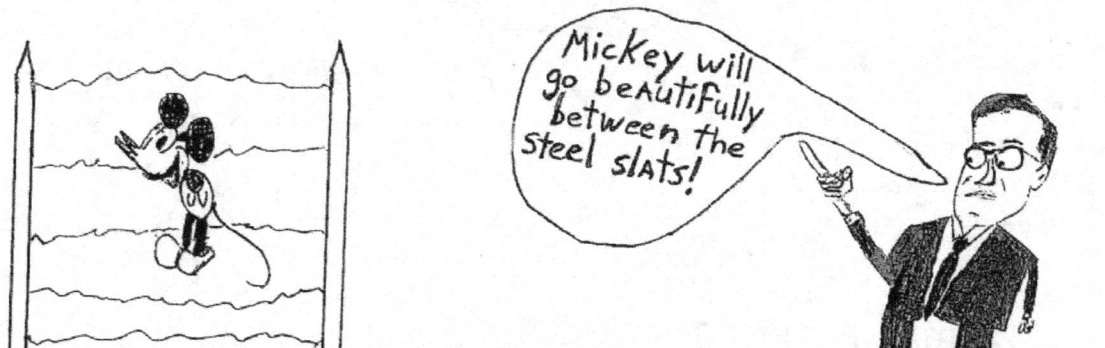

A Tale of Two Versions OF A Meeting Between Trump & Democratic Leaders: Sen. Chuck Schumer Claims That President Had A Frustrated Outburst During Their Meeting & VP Mike Pence Denies It Saying: He "Passed Out Candy" How It Might Have Gone... Jan. 9, 2019

Trump Says He Is Not Concerned About His Former Personal Attorney, Michael Cohen, AKA "The Fixer" Testifying To House Oversight And Reforn Committee On Feb. 7, 2019 - As The Ghost of President Nixon Returns To The White House Lawn

January 10, 2019

Enjoyed your RAT tweet! Never let the rats get to you. I didn't! F_____ tapes!

I'm not worried about it At All

Possible G Rated Version OF President Trump's Address To The Nation On Border "Crisis" To Make His Case For Building A Border Wall Never Broadcasted Leaving Out Assault, Sex Crimes, And Violent Killings: Out of <u>Harry Potter</u> World... January 10, 2018

My Fellow Americans. Tonight, I Am speaking to you because there is A growing humanitarian And security crisis at our southern border. Every day customs And border patrol agents encounter members of Dumbledore's Army trained in duelling At Hogwarts School of Witchcraft!

G RATED
FOR
General Audiences

Secretary of State Mike Pompeo Describes Trump's Decision to Withdraw American Troops From Syria As "Incredibly Clear" And Basically A "Tactical Change" Jan. 12, 2019 Along With Past Support From Sen. Lindsey Graham & Russian President Vladimir Putin

Putin Welcoming U.S. Withdrawal From Syria A day After Trump basically had declared complete victory over ISIS by U.S. Forces.

Sen. Lindsey Graham on His Talk With Trump About Withdrawing U.S. Forces From Syria...

The withdrawal of U.S. troops doesn't change efforts to destroy the Islamic State (ISIS) in Iraq & Syria or pressure on Iran. Middle East goals remain the SAME.

U.S. Withdrawal From Syria is correct because U.S. Forces Are no longer needed.

We talked About Syria And he told me some things I didn't know that made me Feel A lot better About where We're headed in Syria...

What Trump Said In Response To A Reporter's Question About The Washington Post Report That Trump, In An Effort To Conceal Details of His Talks With Putin, Took Possession At Least Once of The Notes Of His Own Interpreter AND What Trump Might Have Been Thinking... January 14, 2019 As He Departs White House...
It's a lot of fake news. That was a very good meeting. I have those meetings, one-on-one, with all leaders, including the president of China, and the prime minister of Japan.
And you'll never get those f_____ reports either!
That should get these reporters on my terrific Trade Truce with China and Fantastic Trade Deal with Japan!

Trump's Possible Frustration Over Moderate House Democrats Not Showing Up For His Shut Down Lunch Invitation Because Of Their Expectation They Were On The Menu. Focusing On The Oval Office GrandFather Clock... Jan. 15, 2019

Where Are those Dems! It's 1:30 Already! And All I'm hearing is tick-tock, tick-tock From this grandFather clock! Lyin James Comey Many times made up stories using, this clock! This f_____ clock goes to ISIS in Syria!

The White House At Work To Peel OFF Rank-And-File Democrats From the Party
Leadership To Pick Up Votes For Trump's Border Wall   January 16, 2019

WANTED: DEMS FOR TRUMP WALL
1. MUST SUPPORT INDEFINITE GOVERNMENT SHUTDOWN
2. MUST BE LOYAL TO PRESIDENT REGARDLESS OF AMERICAN HARDSHIPS
3. MUST BE WILLING TO BLAME THEIR FELLOW DEMOCRATS FOR THE SHUTDOWN
4. MUST BE WILLING TO PUT HEAT ON PELOSI FOR ASKING FOR DELAY IN PRESIDENT TRUMP'S STATE OF UNION

Trump's Personal Attorney, Rudy Giuliani Does Huge Reversal In The Wake Of Paul Manafort Admitting He Gave Polling Data To Russians On the 2016 Election. January 17, 2019 And A Possible Additive To The Saga Giuliani Might Have Been Considering...

I never said there was no collusion between Russia and members of the Trump campaign in 2016. But only that the President himself was not involved in collusion.

Because the only interaction then candidate Trump had with Russian Ambassador Sergey Kislyak and Paul Manafort together was at Trump Tower where they just played the game of blindman's bluff!

Trump's Nominee, William Barr To Become Attorney General And Oversee Mueller's Investigation Argues That Mueller Should **NOT** Be Allowed To Demand That Trump Be Questioned By The Special Counsel's Office About "Alleged Obstruction" Related To His 2017 Firing Of FBI Director James Comey. Yet When Questioned By MN Sen. Amy Klobachar Barr States Repeatedly The Need For "Specific Facts."

To support His Above Argument Barr solely writes in A Memo... A president has the constitutional right to Fire Any subordinate he chooses.

Barr At His Confirmation Hearing Being Questioned By MN Senator Amy Klobachar   January 17, 2019

Sen. Amy Klobachar

IF A president told A witness not to cooperate with An investigation or hinted At A pardon would that be obstruction of Justice?

I'd have to know the specific Facts.

Hon. William P. Barr

Trump JAN. 19 2019 → Offering Protection For Undocumented Immigrants Brought To The United States When They Were Children In Exchange For Funding For His Border Wall And Candidate Trump In 2015 Talking Of Rescinding (DACA) Deferred Action For Childhood Arrivals With Chuck Todd

Jan. 19, 2019

This is A common sense compromise both parties should embrace. The radical left can never control our borders. I will never let it happen.

Sept. 5, 2015

They have to go! We will do it. And we will expedite it so they can come back in. Chuck in 4 years you're goin to be saying... What a great job you've done...President TRUMP!

Bring them back in. Sounds like A David Copperfield Magic Show

Trump HAS BeAutiFul DreAM About BAsicALLy Being Pelosi's TrAvel Agent On Her Trip To Visit Troops In AFghAnistAn In The WAKe OF Upending Her Trip There On A MilitAry PlAne And suggesting She could MAKe Her Journey There by Flying CommerciAl One DAy APter She Suggested Trump Postpone His StAte OF the Union Address... JAn. 19, 2019

TRUST ME NANcy! AFghAnistAn is going to be FANtAstic!

MOTEL 6 FT. UNDER

You Are Flying MADAGASCAR Airlines And StAying two nights At the JAlAlAbAd Motel 6 FT. Under!

Trump's Personal Attorney, Rudy Giuliani Says His Moscow Trump Tower Comment That The President May Have Been Involved In Conversations To Build The Tower Up Until Election Day 2016 Were Hypothetical And Not Intended To Convey Fact: Below A Possible Future Giuliani Hypothetical Explanation Of That Hypothetical Comment. To Defend the President...

January 23, 2019

I said President Trump's conversations were hypothetical because he may have been having those Moscow Trump Tower conversations with only himself. Without any Russian Involvement. And therefore his conversations would have had no real world impacts.

Trump's Former Personal Attorney AKA The Fixer, Michael Cohen Postpones House Testimony
Due to Reported "Threats Against His Family" From Trump & Giuliani... As Giuliani Fears
His Tombstone Will Say, "He Lied for Trump": Below A New Possibility...

January 23, 2019

Trump Has Fantastic Dream Of Delivering His "Great Speech" Before Partial Government Shutdown Ends
At Outside Capitol
January 24, 2019

Mr. Vice President, Members of Congress. From this Mighty U.S. Tank that symbolizes my clear vision + righteous Mission. I can tell you the Truth... Which is we have Made America great Again. Now this here GREAT Speech!

Trump's Commerce Secretary Wilbur Ross Saying Federal Workers Who Have No Money To Buy Food During Government Shutdown Should Borrow From Banks Compared To Marie Antoinette, Bride of France's King Louis XVI Who Around 1789, When Being Told That Her French Subjects Had No Bread Supposedly Said "Let Them EAT CAKE": Trump's Response Compared To The Possible French King's:

January 24, 2019

Wilbur was trying to say that local banks know who these people are when they go for groceries. And they will work along with these federal employees and help them out.

Around 1789

Marie was trying to say that her subjects should eat larger desserts if they feel hungry after their meals.

President Donald Trump Announces Deal Reached To End Government Shutdown And Basically Claims A 99.9 Percent Victory... January 25, 2019
.1 Percent
The President Left OUT→
A tentative deal has been reached to temporarily end the shutdown.
Congress has Finally + Fully acknowledged that having barriers, Fencing or Walls - or Whatever is important.
No matter where you go... Walls Work. Israel's wall is 99.9 percent successful. Except for this HOT AIR BALLOON INCIDENT...

Trump's Top Advisor Mick Mulvaney Being Asked If the President Was Prepared to Enter Yet Another Government Shutdown If His Demands For Funding For the Wall He Wants Are NOT Met And Afghanistan President Ashraf Ghani's Possible Quiet Thoughts... January 27, 2019

FACE NATION

Yeah, I think he ACTUALLY is!

Wonder if Trump would do A third shutdown to build my presidential palace WALL! Make A nice U.S. FAREWELL Present!

Trump's Acting Attorney General Who Trump Had Claimed Was Hired Because He Knows the "Inner Workings" of the Mueller Investigation: When Asked If He Knows of Anything Damaging to the President In the Mueller Report: What He Said And What He Did NOT Say... January 28, 2019

Trump's Tweet Below About the Polar Vortex Applied To A Future Campaign 2020 Rally In Chicago Where the Mercury Plunged to 21 Degrees Below Zero

Donald J. Trump @realDonaldTrump
In the beautiful Midwest, wind chill temperatures are reaching minus 60 degrees, the coldest ever recorded. In coming days, expected to get even colder. People can't last outside even for minutes. What the hell is going on with Global Warming? Please come back fast, we need you!

January 28, 2019

MAKE AMERICA WARM AGAIN

FOR 2020 VOTE TRUMP

Remember back in January of 2019 when it was colder here than Antarctica! Trust me! Global Warming is like a warm blanket on a cold night. This freezing Chicago Abominable Snowman needed a Hot Chocolate.

Trump Says Afghanistan Peace Talks Are Proceeding Well In the Face of the Afghan Leader Calling For Direct Talks With Insurgents, But Militants Still Refusing to Meet With Him...   January 30, 2019

Afghanistan peace talks are proceeding well..

I call on insurgents to begin serious talks and embrace peace.

Trump On Face The Nation Being Asked: Why Don't Facts Influence Your Opinions, If Those Facts Change? And— And Your Director Of National Intelligence Said 'ISIS' Still Has Strongholds In Iraq And Syria... February 3, 2019

What-- you're -- you're going to Always have is pockets of something. You're going to have people, like this one-Armed Man who blew up A restaurant here...

Trump Says His Administration Has Done An Incredible Job With Syria: You Have Very Little ISIS And the Caliphate Is Almost Knocked Out - FACE THE NATION, Feb. 3, 2019

The Possible 1 Percent Trump Never Spoke of ↓

We will be Announcing in the not too distant future 100 percent of the Caliphate which is the Area - the land - the Area - 100. We're at 99 percent right now, we'll be at 100. When we Knock out this ISIS Mister Hot Shine Car Wash.

Trump On Face The Nation Against Advice of His National Security Team Determined
To Pull U.S. Troops Out of Syria & Afghanistan: And Argues... February 3, 2019 We CAN Go BACK FAST!
And Doesn't Argue...

This is a strategic
repositioning. Some
troops leaving Syria
will go to our fantastic
Al-Assad Air Base. They
will be in
watchful waiting
over ISIS!

Iran   Afghanistan

Al-Assad
Air Base
Iraq

Doesn't Argue... Our
huge cargo planes can fly very
fast to avoid the Iranian surface-to-air Missile System. TO GET BACK TO Afghanistan!

Trump At His Second State of the Union Speech On North Korea And V.P. Mike Pence's Quiet Thoughts of Praise For the President's Diplomatic Achievements February 5, 2019

Trump Lashes Out At House Intelligence Committee Chairman Adam Schiff In Good Part Because Schiff's Committee Hired A Former National Security Council (NSC) Staffer And Announced An Intense Investigation of Him In Below Tweet

Donald J. Trump ✓
@realDonaldTrump

... The Dems and their committees are going "nuts". The Republicans never did this to President Obama, there would be no time left to run government. I hear other committee heads will do the same thing. Even stealing people who work at White House! A continuation of Witch Hunt!   6:26 AM Feb. 7, 2019

<u>Possible Future Trump Tweet</u>... If the Dems want to steal people who work at the White House... They can take my physician. Who is nuts about me losing weight. And got me this F _ _ _ _ _ BowFlex Treadclimber, That I am donating to Schiff's Witch Hunt Committee...

Trump's Acting Attorney General Matthew Whitaker Basically Tells Democrats In His Congressional Testimony On Mueller Probe That He Never Talked With Trump About It But Refused To Recuse Himself From Overseeing It... Like Jeff Bo Did, Trump's Former Attorney General, Jeff Sessions)... Below What Whittaker Seemed To Be Using As Evasion Strategy And His Possible Thoughts... February 8, 2019

I won't detail any discussions with the President on the Mueller Investigation. Anyway I'm likely to be in this job for only Another Four or Five days...

These Assholes Are trying to MAKE ME LOSE My Four or Five days... And be lampooned AS MR. CLEAN YOUR DESK OUT!

Trump's Acting Chief of Staff Mick Mulvaney Says President Has POTS of Money He Can Use For Wall Without An Emergency Declaration February 11, 2019: With Possible Future Justification For Plan

We have a plan to get pots of money from disaster relief programs like flood control, Department of Defense funds for family housing and disaster relief programs for Puerto Rico.
This will protect the country from further National Security Emergencies. Like if the President needs a "White House Wall"!

Trump Stuck Between Hard-Core Supporters And Republican Leaders Who Know
The Majority of Americans Are Opposed to the Wall & Another Shutdown Declares Himself
"NOT HAPPY" At Cabinet Meeting In WH Feb. 12, 2019:

Am I happy at first glance?
The Answer is no, I'm not. I'm
not happy. But AM I happy with
where we're going? I'M thrilled.
Because we're supplementing
things and moving things around
And we're doing things that are
FANTASTIC And taking from less
important Areas... LIKE...

Disaster Relief For Hurricanes &
WildFires In United States

Trump In Below Tweet Boasts In His Own Trumpish Language That the Senate Intelligence Committee Has Concluded: No Collusion Between Trump Campaign And Russia

 Donald J. Trump
@realDonaldTrump

The Senate Intelligence Committee:
THERE IS NO EVIDENCE OF
COLLUSION BETWEEN THE TRUMP
CAMPAIGN AND RUSSIA!
5:58 AM - Feb. 13, 2019: In Trump Language

Tweet translated From Trumpish to English basically means... At this point in the investigation they haven't found any rats that talked about collusion... NO COLLUSION!

Trump In Below Tweet Boasts In His Own Trumpish Language That the Senate Intelligence Committee Has Concluded: No Collusion Between Trump Campaign and Russia

Donald J. Trump
@realDonaldTrump

The Senate Intelligence Committee:
THERE IS NO EVIDENCE OF
COLLUSION BETWEEN THE TRUMP
CAMPAIGN AND RUSSIA!
5:58 AM -Feb. 13, 2019: In Trump Language

Tweet translated From Trumpish to English basically means... At this point in the investigation they haven't found any rats that talked about collusion... NO COLLUSION!

Senate Republican Leader Mitch McConnell Basically Says To Get Trump To Sign A Funding Bill That Will Prevent Another Government Shutdown And Avoid Further Political Damage To The Republican Brand. He Will Support Trump Declaring A national emergency To Bypass Congressional Approval And To Siphon Billions From Federal Coffers to Build WALL

Feb. 14, 2019

I just had An opportunity to speak with President Trump. He is prepared to sign the bill. He will be issuing A national emergency declaration. I indicated to him I will support the National Emergency.

That is the National Emergency of A Shutdown Fever epidemic. That could have been Fatal to our Republican Party!

Trump In Rose Garden Address On His Emergency Declaration Says "I've Already Done A Lot of Wall For the Election, 2020." Republican Rep. Jim Jordan Says "The one thing we don't fund is the one Issue We All Campaigned on - A Border Security Wall - And that is not in the legislation."

Feb. 15, 2019

I could do the wall over a longer period of time. I didn't need to do this, but I'd rather do it much faster. And I don't have to do it for the election, I've already done a lot of wall for the election, 2020.

The See-Through Fencing Authorized Under Current Law...
Migrants Climbing Border Fence: Dec.4,2018

Trump's Fantastic Dream Following His National Emergency Speech Where He Predicted   Feb. 18, 2018
After Bad Rulings "We'll end up in the Supreme Court"
And We Will Win There!

Trump Tweets Out Bathroom-Themed Dig At Former FBI Deputy Director Andrew McCabe. In Accordance With Below Tweet Former FBI Director James Comey Saying His Last Farewell After Being Fired to Then FBI Deputy Director Andrew McCabe

Donald J. Trump
@realDonaldTrump

Remember this, Andrew McCabe didn't go to the bathroom without the approval of Leakin' James Comey!

10:26 PM - Feb. 18, 2019

Trump According To A New York Times Report May Have Tried To Get Acting Attorney General Whitaker To Put A Trump Ally In Charge of the Investigation of His Former Personal Attorney Michael Cohen. Given the Above And the Saga of Jeff Sessions AKA Mister Magoo... The Below Depicts A Future Trump World Possibility...

Feb. 19, 2019

My second National Emergency Declaration is...ON...the FAKE NEWS Crisis threatening our great country. Effective immediately this fantastic symbol of our democracy will be renamed... The Trump War Department on Fake News Investigations...

THE TRUMP WAR DEPARTMENT ON FAKE NEWS INVESTIGATIONS

Trump, According To New York Times Report Pressured Matthew Whitaker, Then the Acting Attorney General To Exert Control Over Federal Prosecutors In New York. Also Reported Was That Whitaker Told Justice Department Associates That the Prosecutors Needed "Adult Supervision".

Feb. 20, 2019

SOUTHERN DISTRICT OF NEW YORK PROSECUTORS DAY CARE CENTER

Stop crying I'm going to read you this story book tale called The Art of the Deal by our great president, Donald J. Trump

Trump Has Fantastic Dream That His Long Time Friend, David Pecker Publisher of the National Enquirer Got Control of The New York Times. Following the President's Escalating Attacks on the Times. Calling it A "True Enemy of the People." Feb. 21, 2019

The New York Times
A David Pecker Publication

TRUMP SAVES U.S. FROM
NUCLEAR APOCALYPSE AS
NORTH KOREA DENUCLEARIZES

100 PERCENT

Sen. Lindsey Graham Says He Will Vote To Support Trump's Decision To Declare A National Emergency To Get Funding For the WALL. Basically Proclaiming The President Has the Support & Power:

Sen. Lindsey Graham On Taking Away Funds From Building A Middle-School In Kentucky...

I would say it's better For the middle-school Kids in Kentucky to have A secure border. We'll get them the school they need. But right now we've got A national emergency on our hands...

Feb. 22, 2019

Following Republican Sen. Chuck Grassley's Success With His Opening the Senate On Feb. 14, 2019 With A Prayer that President Trump Will Have Wisdom To Sign the Bipartisan Bill On Border Security. Grassley's Possible Prayer For the Trump-Kim Nuclear Talks In Hanoi, Vietnam   Feb. 24, 2019

Let's now pray President Trump's great love for Chairman Kim will make America more secure. Maybe an agreement that North Korea will not fire more ballistic missiles over Japan. And Kim will not order more underground hydrogen bomb tests.

Trump Vows Veto As Democrats Try to Block His Emergency Declaration To Bypass Congress And Get Funding For His Wall...   Feb. 26, 2019

Will I veto it? 100 percent 100 percent. It's Fantastic! Best Adviser, Colonel Sanders here agrees with me! Look at that huge smile! And BUCKET!

KFC

The Trump Adminstration's Tale of Two Threat Levels Regarding North Korea

Donald J. Trump ✓
@realDonald Trump

Secretary of State Mike Pompeo's being
Asked on CNN whether he believes the
Kim regime still poses A nuclear threat
to the World... Feb. 24, 2019

President Trump's Tweet After First Summit...

Just landed - A long trip, but everybody can
now feel much safer than the day I took
office. There is no longer A Nuclear
threat from North Korea. Meeting with
Kim Jong Un was An interesting And very
positive experience. North Korea has
great potential for the future!
4:56 AM - June 13, 2018

Yes- President Trump never said
North Korea was no longer A nuclear
threat; What he said is that efforts
that have been made in Singapore,
this commitment that Chairman Kim
Made, have substantially taken down
the risk to the American people.

Trump Touts North Korea's Potential To Become An "Economic Powerhouse" Ahead Of His Second Summit With Kim Jong Un: Saying June 12, 2018... North Korea's Beaches Would Be Prime Real Estate For Luxury Condos And Glitzy Hotels e.g. Miami Beach's Fountainbleau

Donald J. Trump
@realDonaldTrump

Meeting for breakfast with our Nation's Governors - then off to Vietnam for a very important Summit with Kim Jong Un. With complete Denuclearization, North Korea will rapidly become An Economic Powerhouse. Without it, just more of the same. Chairman Kim will make a wise decision!
7:40 AM - Feb. 25, 2019

North Korea's Continental Climate...
The country is affected by the monsoon circulation: during winter the cold northwest wind of Siberian origin prevails. The rains brought by the summer monsoon can be very abundant and cause flooding.

In summer and in early autumn, the country can be reached by TYPHOONS.

Future Travel Agency Ad
SEE NORTH KOREA!
DON'T MISS MONSOON
LOW SUMMER RATES
NOW AVAILABLE

Trump Says He Does NOT Hold Kim Jong Un Responsible For Otto WArmbier's Death And Believes Kim Did Not Know About the "BAd Things" That Happened To Otto. Otto WAs An American College student Who HAd Been Convicted of Theft of A propAgAndA poster From A North KoreA Hotel in 2016...

Feb. 28, 2019

① Mr. President, Feel very bad About Otto!

② I believe you CHAirMAn Kim!

If there is A Future Trump Tower RyongyAng. Could you hold the PropAgAndA POSTERS!

Some of my very weAlthy guests Are AlwAys taking souvenirs From My FantAstic hotels!

Michael Cohen, Trump's Former Lawyer And Fixer In His Testimony He Gave Before the House Oversight Committee Said Mr. Trump Directed Him to Threaten His High School, His Colleges And the College Board to Never Release Grades or SAT Scores. In May 2015 Before Trump Declared He Was Running For President...

Feb. 28, 2019... Michael Cohen's Next Day Possible Closed Session Testimony On One of those threatening letters He Might Have Sent...

Feb. 28, 2019

Mr. Trump never challenged the Fact that he "graduated first in his class" From Wharton in 1968, which had been widely reported. In 1968 A Pennsylvanian publication Failed to list Mr. Trump on the Wharton Dean's List. Therefore I threatened Wharton with A Billion Dollar Lawsuit!!

Trump Ordering Top-Secret Clearance For Jared Kushner Overruling Concerns of Security Officials And His Own White House Staff Including John Kelly, Then Chief of Staff As The Ghost of Nixon Returns To Support Trump Back In May of 2018 It Is Alleged...

Deputy Attorney General Rod Rosenstein Who Long Oversaw Robert Mueller's Investigation Says That it is Not Always Appropriate For the Government to be Transparent. He Argues that Prosecutors Should Not Level Public Allegations Against People they do NOT Charge And Just Investigate...This could be Setting The Stage For the Justice Department To NOT Disclose Too Much About President Donald Trump... February 25, 2019

There's A Knee-jerk reaction to suggest that we should be Transparent About What we do in government. But there Are A lot of reasons not to be transparent About what we do in GOVERNMENT!

Trump Returns to CPAC Where He Had Spoken Before Becoming President... Igniting Crowd Like Rock Star Bob Dylan

Conservative Political Action Conference

AMERICAN CONSERVATIVE UNION
★ CPAC 2019

This 2019 Album is gonna be number 1!

March 2, 2019

PRESIDENT OF

TRACK LIST   Top 4 From Trump 2019 CPAC Album...
① Jokerman Jeff Sessions Says "I'm going to recuse myself"
② Little Shifty Schiff Blowin In The Wind "I want his Finances"
③ Don't Think Twice, It's All Right... I was only joking About Russia Finding Hillary Clinton's emails
④ The Watchtower Man Who Came 5 Hrs. Early To Photo Nobody At My INAUGURATION

Trump Strongly Implies That the Congressional Testimony of Michael Cohen, His Former Personal Lawyer And Fixer Was Contributory to the Collapse In Nuclear Negotiations With North Korea And Trump's Possible Story...

Donald J. Trump
@realDonaldTrump

For the Democrats to interview in open hearings a convicted liar & fraudster, at the same time as the very important Nuclear Summit with North Korea, is perhaps a new low in American politics and may have contributed to the WALK. Shame!

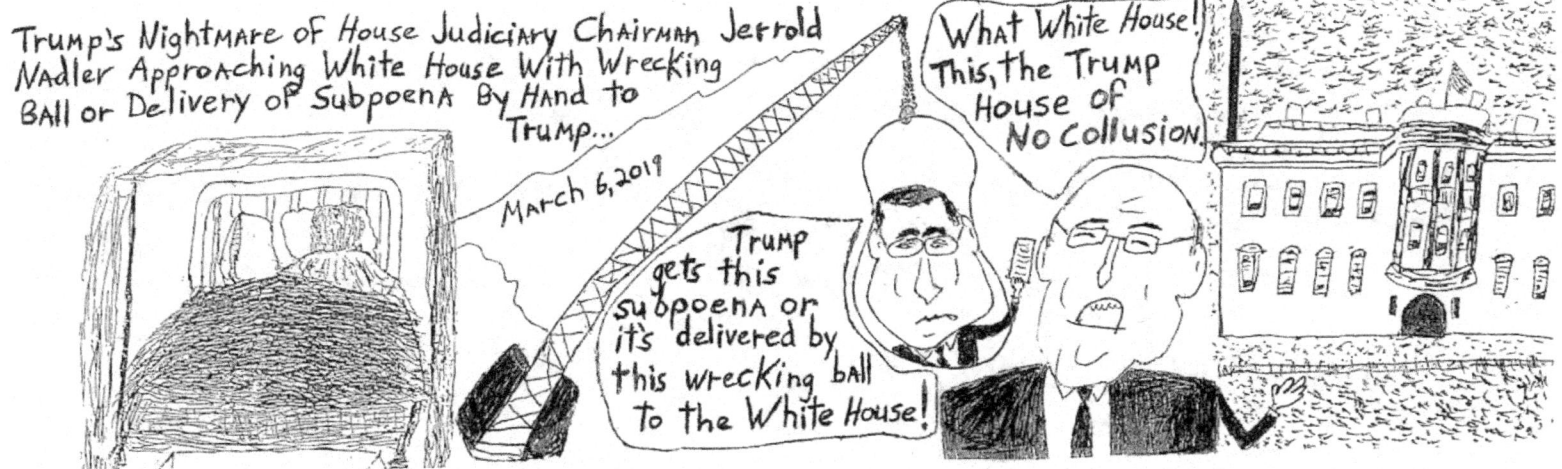

Adam Schiff, Chairman of the House Intelligence Committee Reintroduces The Abuse of the Pardon Prevention Act In An Effort to Prevent Trump And Future Presidents From Abusing Their Pardon Authority And Acting Like A Crime Boss...
March 7, 2019

Nov. 28, 2018... Days After Mueller's team said Manafort had breached his plea Agreement by repeatedly lying to investigators on a variety of topics...

I've never discussed pardoning Paul Manafort, but it's not off the table. Why would I take it off the table?

↓ Possible Addition From today's Manafort Ruling... "He led An otherwise blameless life."

Trump's Fantastic Dream Following the President's FALSE Claim that Manafort's Judge, T.S. Ellis Declared There WAS NO COLLUSION With Russia By Anyone   March 9, 2019

The Allegations of collusion with Russia is FAKE news. And should not be Admitted into Any Court of law. It is a hoax being used by the media to Attack both President Donald Trump And Paul Manafort. Both of these Men who have led blameless lives.

Trump Following A Week Of Democratic Division & Infighting Over A Passed House
Resolution that Broadly Condemned Hate, Racism, & Anti-Semitism Instead Of Specifically
Condemning Past Alleged Anti-Semitic Remarks Questioning the Patriotism Of Some
Jewish Americans Made by Rep. Ilhan Omar... And What He Possibly Was Thinking...
March 8, 2019

Democrats have become An
Anti-Israel And Anti-Jewish
party...

This should help unify the
country Against Democrats.
Without A Traumatic event!
What A Fantastic Message!
This proves the Anti-Wall Dems Are
Anti-Israel too! WALLS WORK!

Trump Sends Congress A Record $4.75 Trillion Budget Plan Calling For Sharp Cuts To Domestic Programs For the 2020 Fiscal Year... Democratic Leaders In Both House & Senate Pronounce the Budget Dead On Arrival As Two Republican Leaders McConnell & Graham of the Senate Say Their Tearful Goodbyes to the Deceased Budget of Trump In Days

March 13, 2019

Trump On New Boeing 737 MAX8 Crashes: Saying That Airplanes Are Becoming Far Too Complex to Fly And That Complexity Creates Danger... As Dozens of Countries Including All EU Member States Have Grounded This New Best Selling

Donald J. Trump ✓ U.S. Made Jet... March 12, 2019
@realDonaldTrump

Airplanes Are becoming Far too complex to fly. Pilots Are no longer needed, but rather computer scientists from MIT. I see it all the time in many products. Always seeking to go one unnecessary step further. Complexity creates danger. And I don't know About you, but I don't want Albert Einstein to be My pilot...

✳ Trump in the Face of mounting pressure said his Administration was ordering Boeing 737 MAX 8 jets grounded pending More information on March 13, 2019

Trump Delivers Remarks From the Oval Office Following the Senate's Vote On March 14, 2019 to Block his Emergency At the Southern Border As He Signs His First Veto Rebuking this Congressional Rejection... A Dozen Republican Senators Voted Against Trump On Principles of Separation of powers And the Bad Precedent it sets for A Future Democratic president To Unilaterally Drive their Agenda... Like A Hypothetical Bernie Sanders Presidency...

My Fellow Americans back in 2016 I said... When we need the best-educated workforce in the world, yes, we are going to make public colleges and universities tuition-free. Today I AM declaring A Work Force National Emergency. Ordering that promise be kept. We will have the most educated work force in the world. This is not A question that needs Congressional Approval! Look At Trump's Meshuggeneh WALL!

Trump Responding to A Question From Breitbart News: Explaining How the American
Left Plays, in Trump's Words, Cuter And Tougher: And What Trump Might Have Held Back...

March 15, 2019

The left plays A tougher game, it's very funny. I actually think that the people on the right Are tougher, but they don't play it tougher.

Okay? I can tell you I have the support of the police, the support of the Military, And the support of the Bikers For Trump...

Some of these Bikers Are of German Ancestry And have Waffen SS Members in their Family tree...

Trump's Ally & Former Acting Attorney General Meets With House Judiciary Chairman Jerry Nadler... During Talks Matthew Whitaker According to Nadler "Did **Not** Deny" that President Trump had Called Him to Talk About "Personnel Decisions" Involving A Federal Investigation Into Hush-Money Payments Made to Two Women Who Alleged They had Affairs With Trump Regarding the Michael Cohen Case... How It Might Have Gone Between Trump & Then Acting Attorney General Whitaker...

March 16, 2019

① Matt, I hope you can see your way clear to putting Geoffrey Berman in charge of the Cohen Investigation. He has Always been a Fantastic U.S. Attorney for Me!

② Can't do it Mr. President!

③ You were hired to stop the illegal Mueller probe! Not to be Mr. Clean!

Trump, Following Below Excerpt From His Tweet In Support of Judge Jeanine Pirro After Her Suspension From Fox News For Saying Anti-Muslim Remarks Has Fantastic Dream of Appointing the Judge to the U.S. Supreme Court Following the Retirement of Justice Ruth Bader Ginsburg...

Donald J. Trump
@realDonaldTrump

March 17, 2019

Bring back [Judge Jeanine.] The Radical Left Democrats, working closely with their beloved partner, the Fake News Media, is using every trick in the book to SILENCE a majority of our country. They have all out campaigns against Fox News hosts who are doing too well. Must stay strong and fight back with vigor. Be strong & prosper, be weak & die!

SUPREMA CORTE

Fantastic Day For America! Bad Day For Fake News Media!

Good Luck to Supreme Court Justice Jeanine!

Trump Tweets General Motors: Demanding It Should Reopen or Sell Its Lordstown, Ohio Chevy Cruze Plant: Fast & Furious... Claiming that "Car Companies Are All coming back to the U.S." And Touting the U.S. Economy As "the envy of All."

Donald J. Trump ☑ 🐦
@realDonald Trump

General Motors and the UAW Are going to start "talks" in September/October. Why wait, start them now! I want jobs to stay in the U.S.A. And want Lordstown (Ohio), in one of the best economies in our history, opened or sold to A company who will open it up Fast! Car companies....

7:37 AM - Mar 18, 2019

Even As Mr. Trump said he talked to Barra, he was calling on GM to reopen its Lordstown plant or find Another owner, while insisting that the Detroit Automaker "must act quickly."

<u>THE ONLY THING TRUMP DID NOT DO</u>↓

General Motors I want this TRUMP Chevy Van built F_____ Fast! HERE!

Trump's Possible Future Meeting With U.S. Sec. of State Mike Pompeo: Given Kim Jong un's Vice Foreign
Minister Recently Said Kim Will Make His Decision Shortly On Future
Missile Test Launches And Suspending Nuclear Talks With the U.S.

A Future Date
In 2019...

Trump Before Leaving White House March 20, 2019 For A Trip To Ohio: And Trump's Possible Thoughts At the Time About Attorney General, William P. Barr's Handling of the Mueller Report In Days to Come...

Trump Blocks Large-Scale Sanctions Against North Korea, Over-ruling His
Own Administration's Experts: Proclaiming that He "likes Chairman Kim"
And "Doesn't Think Sanctions Necessary." Followed By Nicolás Maduro
Asking Himself: Why Can't Trump Like Me? March 23, 2019

Donal J. Trump
@ real Donald Trump

It was announced today by the
U.S. Treasury that additional large
scale Sanctions would be added to
those already existing Sanctions on
North Korea. I have today ordered
the withdrawal of those Additional
Sanctions!

Mar 22, 2019 1:22 PM

Why can't Trump
like ME too?

Trump Following the Release of the Conclusions of the Mueller Investigation has Fantastic Dream About Being An Ancient Roman Emperor Known As, Donald Tiberius Trump... March 26, 2019

Fellow citizens of Rome - Your emperor, Donald Tiberius Trump proclaims... No Collusion, No Obstruction, Complete And TOTAL EXONERATION. The Illegal take down plot against me has failed. We can never let this happen to another Roman Emperor again. People have done evil and treasonous things. They will be given Free tickets to our Colosseum here...

Trump Says The Republican Party Will Become Known As "The Health Care Party" As the Trump Justice Department Under Trump's Attorney General Bill Barr Argues that the Entire Affordable Care Act Should Be Found Unconstitutional. That Would Mean An End to the Private Markets where 15 million Americans Buy Their Coverage, An End to the Expansion of Medicaid, And An End to Protections For People With Pre-existing Conditions... March 26, 2019 As Bill Barr Would Explain It...

The president has given his word that he will not sign a repeal-and-replace package for the Affordable Care Act that does not adequately protect individuals who have pre-existing conditions. And if the court strikes it down the Trump Administration has a "plan B." Which he would make known after the 2020 election.

Trump With Netanyahu Formally Recognizes Israel's Authority Over Golan Heights As Israeli Prime Minister Makes Video For His Election Campaign

March 25, 2019

Trump Happy to Look Like A Hero by Claiming He Restored Funding to the Special Olympics. After it had Appeared the Education Secretary was responsible for the massive cuts. Betsy Devos who had Supported the cuts then does A 180 turn Following Trump... March 27, 2019

Mr. President, see you At the Special Olympics After my broken legs get better!

Trump Tells Fox News' Sean Hannity That Attorney General William Barr "is a great gentlemen" And "Had he been there initially, this all would not have happened." What happened... By virtue of the Authority vested in me As Acting Attorney General Robert S. Mueller III is Appointed to serve As Special Counsel For the United States Department of Justice... Rod J. Rosenstein ↓ Would Have Happened...

The Trump Administration Addresses the Confusion Caused by the White House Cover Up For Trump Rogue Tweet Reversing North Korea Sanctions. Below the Unknowned Administration Official Who Demanded Total Anonymity...

March 27, 2019

THE WHITE HOUSE

The president was actually talking About sanctions that had yet to be Announced. Not the new sanctions that had just been Announced a day earlier before the president's rogue tweet. No Additional sanctions will be pursued.

Trump At Michigan Rally Declares "Russia Hoax" Dead And Cites This Week
As One Of the Best In American History... March 28, 2019

My foes failed to overturn the
results of the 2016 election and
are no longer fans of special
counsel Robert Mueller. The Russia
hoax is finally dead. The collusion
delusion is over. Those who pushed
the Russia Investigation have now
got big problems.
America just had one of
it best weeks ever.
Like the week of July 4, 1776
when the Continental Congress
Approved the Declaration of
Independence!

SEAL PRESIDENT OF UNITED STATE
U.S.

Adam Schiff, House Intelligence Committee Chairman Hits BACK HARD With "Collusion" Case After Republicans Call For His Resignation In WAKE oF Mueller Report's Release: And WhAt Schiff Did Not Say... March 28, 2019

You Might say it's OK For Attorney General Bill Barr to hand us A 4 Page Mueller Report For DUMMIES. But I Don't Think It's OK.

IN SEARCH OF JUSTICE AFTER MUELLER...
TO CATCH A SPY WHO CAME IN DURING THE
EARLY STAGE OF RUSSIA PROBE...

R. Friedman

Attorney General Barr Says In New Letter that he Expects A Redacted Version of the Special Counsel's Findings to be Made Public by Mid-April. Saying that Mueller will Assist Him In Redacting... Grand Jury Proceeding, Intelligence Sources And Methods, Details of Ongoing Investigations, And Information that would "unduly Infringe personal privacy And reputational interests of peripheral third parties"...   March 29, 2019

Trump's Possible Thoughts As he suddenly Says Public Should See Mueller's Final Redacted Report...

I don't mind, I mean, Frankly, I told the House, if you want, let them see it.

Barr Knows that I don't give A shit About the privacy And reputation of All those losers. He Knows to redact Any stuff that could be used by the Dems And Deep State to overturn the 2016 Election. Say, when Mueller goes to the bathroom!

WH Acting Chief of Staff Mick Mulvaney Attacks Obama Care Without A Plan to Replace It Except to Say "We're going to do the samething we did with Taxes"...
March 31, 2019

Our plan is that Obama Care is unconstitutional. And the president campaigned on getting rid of all of it. Therefore, the Administration is seeking that Federal Courts strike down all of it. We are going to give people the choices they want, the Affordability they need, and quality they deserve. We will use the same legislative process that got us the tremendous Trump Tax Cut Plan through Congress. It got my friend the Rolls Royce he deserved!

MY 2018 TAX Cut

Trump's Top White House Aide Kellyanne Conway On Fox News Sunday With Chris Wallace Argues For President's Repeated False Claims that he was totally Exonerated by Special Counsel Robert Mueller's Russia Investigation & Conway's Possible Final Thoughts...

March 31, 2019

① The special counsel cleared the president on collusion, absolutely no question about it. But he especially did not clear him on the question of obstruction, so why is the president telling Americans something that is not true?

② Well the president is probably comparing that report, and the ultimate conclusions of no collusion, no conspiracy, no contact with any Russians at a campaign to people saying we would cheat, lie, steal or talk to any Russians. And there's nowhere in the Barr report that said the president obstructed justice.

③ Well there is no Barr report, Barr just summarized Mueller, and Mueller said that it did not exonerate him.

FOX NEWS SUNDAY

④ This Chris Wallace can not understand Alternative Facts!

Chapter II April 2019 - June 2019

Trump Says He Will Reveal His "Really Great" Health-Care Plan — After 2020
Election... April 1, 2019

Donald J. Trump ✓
@realDonaldTrump

... Are developing a really great Health Care Plan with
Far lower premiums (cost) + deductables than
Obama Care. In other words it will be far less
expensive & much more usable than Obama Care.
Vote will be taken right after the Election when
Republicans hold the Senate & win..... 10:23 PM — April 1, 2019

Future Donald J. Trump IF Dems
Win the Senate in 2020...

Donald J. Trump ✓
@realDonald Trump

The American people no longer
deserve my really great Health-Care
Plan. Today I proclaim Obama-Care
Unconstitutional. Still want Obama-
Care! Go to a Witch Doctor!

The White House Whistle-Blower Who Returned To Work After Committee
Released Her Deposition that At Least 25 Employees Who Were Denied
Security Clearances by Career Staff Members Had Been Overruled.
Her Possible White House Reassignment... April 2, 2019

Attorney General Barr Gets the Idea of How to Defend His Disputed Four-Page Summary of the Mueller Report While Eating a Package of Thomas Bagels for Breakfast...
April 4, 2019

CONTAINS WHEAT, SOY MADE IN A BAKERY THAT MAY ALSO USE MILK, EGG, WALNUTS.

THOMAS BAGELS

Barr's Statement Excerpt

Every page of Mueller's report was marked that it may contain grand jury material and therefore could not immediately be released.

Trump Picks Former Pizza Magnate & Presidential Candidate Herman Cain For Federal Reserve Board Where He Will Help Set Interest Rates... Trump Has Been A Critic Of the Fed's Rate Hikes... Possible Cain Response... April 5, 2019

Remember my 9-9-9 Plan From 2012. For the Fed I have A Zero, Zero, Zero Plan. That offers zero interest rate hikes, zero economic principles designed to cool economy and control inflation, and zero cheese Free Pizza that does not taste good and lowers Moral and cardiovascular disease.

Trump Characterizes the Security Breach At His Mar-A-Lago Resort By A Chinese Woman Carrying Thumb Drive With Malware As "Just A Fluke" Incident, As China's President Xi Jinping Soon to Meet With Trump Reacts... April 4, 2019

Trump Directs His White House to Maneuver to Block the Release of His Tax Returns And Appears to Imply to Include the Department of Justice under Attorney General Barr As Part of His Great Effort... Trump In Oval Office When Asked About Democrats Request For 6 years of His Personal And Business Tax Returns... How Trump Views Department of Justice... April 4, 2019

They'll speak to my lawyers and they'll speak to the Attorney General.

TRUMP JUSTICE DEPARTMENT of LEGAL DEFENSE

Trump Makes Unfounded Rebuke of Wind Power Claiming that the Noise Produced by Windmills "Causes Cancer" And According to the Daily Beast, Trump Has talked About Writing A Tell-All Memoir Once He's Out of Office   April 5, 2019
How It Would Go If Trump Started A Charity For Victims of Windmill Cancer...

Good evening... I'm Donald J. Trump, Former president of the United States. Who would still be president if not for massive voter fraud. Tonight I am asking you to pledge whatever you can to my Trump Windmill Cancer Foundation. Together we can do FANTASTIC things to wipe out this horrible disease. Along with all these kind of windmills!

White House Acting Chief of Staff Mick Mulvaney Takes On Additional Title as WH Fortune Teller As Treasury Says it will Miss Democrats' Deadline For Turning Over Trump Tax Returns By This Wednesday...April 10, 2019

April 7, 2019

Democrats will never see Trump's Tax Returns

Trump's Firing of Sec. of Homeland Security Kirstjen Nielsen On Sunday Followed By Trump's Monday Afternoon Massacre of the DHS's Senior Management Leaves the Below Head of its Mailroom In Charge of Protecting the United States... April 9, 2019

How does it feel to be the first Acting, Acting Secretary of Homeland Security in the history of the United States?

Treasury Secretary Steve Mnuchin On Capitol Hill Says He Will
"Follow the law" On the Request to Supply Trump's Tax Returns Wednesday...
But Fails to Indicate if he would Actually Comply with the Request...

April 9, 2019

I will comply with the law. I have not promised to Authorize the IRS to supply the returns.

THE LAW... A 1924 statute states the Treasury Department "shall furnish" returns when requested The IRS is part of the Treasury Department.

The Conclusion... When Mnuchin refers to Following the law. He does not Mean U.S. LAW. He means Trump LAW.

Trump's Attorney General, Bill Barr Pressed And Put to the **Test** by House Democrat Rep. Cartwright... IF your **DOJ's** Efforts Are Successful in Striking Down the Affordable Care Act Millions of Americans Would lose their Health Care... Has your Justice Department Analyzed All the Bad Impacts...

April 9, 2019

The president has made it clear that he has a plan to replace the Affordable Care Act. And if you think it's an outrageous position, you have **nothing** to **worry** about.

Trump's Care Plan... To be released after the 2010 presidential election. And then to blame his own Republicans for not working on his rally point that the GOP will come up with a "terrific" plan.

Trump's Attorney General, Bill Barr when Asked if the White House has seen the Mueller Report Says..."I'm landing the plane right now" And "I'm not getting into the details of the process until the plane is on the ground"... Then Crashes the Plane by Saying... Spying on Trump Campaign "did occur," without providing Any Evidence...

April 10, 2019

Mr. Barr should have Known better. He was A great And FANTASTIC legal scholar

Trump: On the Mueller Investigation April 11, 2019

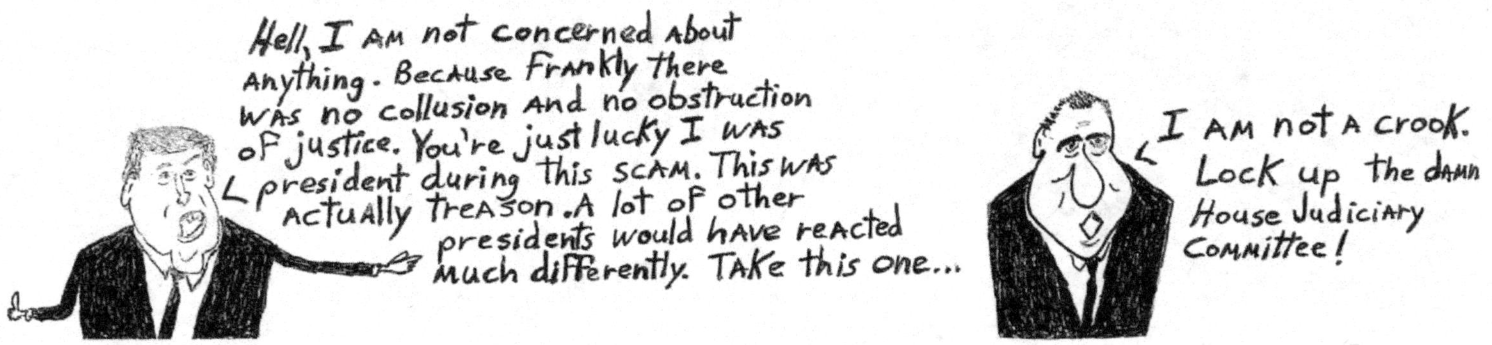

Deputy Attorney General Defends Attorney General Barr's Summary of the Mueller Report: As Trump Hears the Words of Rod Rosenstein   April 11, 2019 With Vice-President Mike Pence...

He's being as forthcoming as he can, and so this notion that he's trying to mislead people, I think, is just completely bizarre.

Hear that Mike! Nancy Pelosi is completely bizarre!

Trump's Nightmare About Driving A Bus of Undocumented Immigrants To the "Sanctuary City" Of San Francisco Only to Find They Receive A Big Welcome...
April 13, 2019

WELCOME TO YOUR SANCTUARY

TRUMP MIGRANT BUSING TOURS

Next bus goes to Barbra Streisand's Estate in Malibu!

Trump Reportedly Offered Kevin McAleenan, Now Acting Homeland Security Secretary A Pardon IF He Were Sent to Jail For Having Border Agents Block Asylum Seekers From Entering the U.S. In Defiance oF U.S. Law... How It Might Have Gone At The Border... April 12, 2019

⑤ I have eternal power over history! There will be a huge heroic statue of you at the grand entrance to my Trump Presidential Library!

① Here's the deal! The numbers on illegal border crossing are in the shit house. I want that {expletive deleted} border closed and asylum seekers blocked!

③ You will be out in 5 minutes. I'll pardon you immediately!

Mr. President ② I could go to JAIL!

④ But Mr. President What About MY NAME In HISTORY!

Trump Who Owned the Trump Shuttle Airline From 1989-1992 Tweets Advice
to Boeing On Its Grounded & Troubled Boeing 737 MAX ... April 15, 2019

Donald J. Trump ✓
@realDonaldTrump

Introducing Boeing's 36-24-36 Topless Lounge

What do I Know about branding, maybe
nothing (but I did become President)
but if I were Boeing, I would FIX
the Boeing 737 MAX, Add some Additional
great Features, & REBRAND the plane with
A new name. →

Trump's Tax Lawyer Compares Democratic Lawmakers Wanting President's
Tax Returns to the Government Targeting African-American Civil Rights
Leaders Taxes During the Height of Segregation In a Letter to the
Treasury Department... April 15, 2019

"Congress motives do Matter under the Constitution. Take the Constitution's
ban on intentional racial discrimination For example. What if during the height
of the civil-rights movement, the Democrat-controlled House tried to
intimidate African-American Leaders by Requesting their Tax Returns?"

Conclusion... Donald J. Trump's rights as an American White Nationalist
Leader can not be infringed upon because he happens to be the
President of the United States...

Trump Aides Worry Mueller Report Will Expose Them As "Leaks" And Some
White House Staffers Are Reportedly Having "breakdown-level Anxiety" that
the Mueller Report Will Out them As Sources of Embarrassing Information...
An Emotionally Upset Staffer Tries Psychiatric Counseling... April 17, 2019

The Trump/Barr Puppet Show Hours Before the Redacted Mueller Report is Released to Anyone in Congress... The Message Barr Will Deliver At Morning News Conference... With An Appearance of Deputy Atty. Gen. Rod Rosenstein Who For the Most Part Will Likely Dummy Up... April 18, 2019 9:30AM

① Good Morning... First Question...

③ The only thing I bake Are Frozen Meat balls Mozzarella Cheese pizzas! The Cold FACT IS I WANT THE FACTS TO SPEAK WITHOUT ME!

② Mr. Attorney General how do you respond to people who say you Are not Allowing the Facts of the Mueller report to speak For themselves. But instead Are trying to bake the report to the benefit of the White House?

Mueller Interviewing Barr Following Attorney General's Statement... "The Trump Admistration was cooperative about sharing campaign documents, providing unfettered access, instructed witnesses to testify in the investigation, and asserted no privilege or privacy claims. All of this is evidence of non-corrupt motives" _How It Would Have Gone_... April 20, 2019

What's the point of all this crap! Since Trump ordered White House counsel Don McGahn to fire me. And then to top it off pressured McGahn to deny reports he was ever asked to fire me!

At that moment President Trump was frustrated and angered by his sincere belief the investigation was undermining his presidency. He only asked Don McGahn to forget the whole thing out of his sincerity in wanting the TRUTH!

Trump Hanging Up On Then Attorney General Jeff Sessions After Lambasting him for NOT Protecting Him Against the Appointment of A Special Counsel And Scarlett O'Hara Quote from "Gone With the Wind"...

Oh my God, this is terrible. This is the end of my Presidency. I'm f---ed!

Maybe not! Someday I'll find Another Attorney General who will do his job And protect me! After All, tomorrow is Another day!

April 20, 2019

Trump's Attorney, Rudy Giuliani Says "Nothing Wrong" With Taking Information From Russia After Mueller Report, Saying Possibly ill-Advised but not illegal On CNN's "State of the Union" As Putin Watches From Kremlin Office April 21, 2019

Comrade Stalin! Check out our Comrade Rudy on CNN!

CNN Americans had A right L to Know About Dem. emails hacked by Russians.

A Possible Trump Future Scenario Given the U.S. Nuclear System is Designed to Respond to A Commander in Chief's Launch Order Instantaneously And An Anonymous Trump Official Claims Insiders Are "Thwarting" Him. And this Resistance is Being Forced Out... eg Former U.S. Secretary of Defense 'Mad Dog' Mattis Who Trump reportedly Called "Moderate Dog"...
April 21, 2019

Mr. President I took this job to save the world! Please don't NUKE North Korea!

Sometimes even true love relationships don't work out!

Trump At White House Easter Tradition Event Posing With the Easter Bunny On Balcony of WH Considers the Rabbit As His Next Attorney General...

April 22, 2019

Trump Has Fantastic Dream About the U.S. Constitution Following His Tweets That Had Argued
He Would "First head to the U.S. Supreme Court" to Stop An Impeachment Drive. And A Reputable
Constitutional Law Professor Saying the Supreme Court Would Want Nothing to do With A
Legal Challenge Like That. And Constitutional Experts Saying Impeachment Begins In the House
And Is Followed By A Trial In the Senate IF the House Votes to Impeach...

Donald J. Trump ✓
@realDonaldTrump

The Mueller Report despite being written
by Angry Democrats And Trump Haters,
And with unlimited money behind it
($35,000,000), didn't lay a glove on me.
I DID NOTHING WRONG. IF the
partisan Dems ever tried to Impeach,
I would First head to the U.S. Supreme
Court. Not only...... 8:10 AM - Apr 24, 2019

Acting White House Chief of Staff Mick Mulvaney Says: "Don't Recall"
Telling Aides to Keep Discussions About Russian Election Meddling Away
From Trump. Because Mr. Trump still Equated Any TALK of MALig'n Russian
Election Activity with Questions About the LegitMAcy of his Victory...
Followed by Trump Congratulating Mulvaney For his Loyalty... April 24, 2019

Mick... Thank you for not
Mentioning that thing About
some people trying to take
AwAY My great election victory!
That showed FANTASTIC
loyalty!

I don't recall
Mr. President!

Trump Welcomes "Sleepy Joe" Biden to "Nasty" Presidential Race in 2020. Repeating His July 2018 Remark. That he "Dreams" About Biden Running After Challenging Biden to A Fist Fight Following Biden's Comment that "IF [he And Trump] were in high School, I'd take him behind the gym And beat the hell out of him." The Dream Trump Has. And His Take On It...

April 25, 2019

Trump's Take In Future Tweet

Donald J. Trump
@realDonaldTrump

Crazy Joe Biden tried to act like a tough guy. Now he knows me. After going down fast and hard. TRUE AND FANTASTIC DREAM!

Trump Speaking At NRA Meeting Accuses Democrats & U.S. Intelligence of Using the Mueller Investigation As An Attempted "OVERTHROW."
April 26, 2019

① Mr. Trump you have two hours to leave the White House. Or I will be back with TANKS!

③ They sure tried for a coup, it didn't work out so well: Spying, surveillance. Trying for an overthrow. And we caught them, we caught them. And I didn't need a gun for that one, did I?

② No collusion and no conclusion about whether Mr. Trump illegally obstructed justice...

NRA   NRA

Given Trump's Former White House Counsel Dan McGahn Now Appears To Be the President's Biggest Threat Towards A Possible Route to Impeachment On Allegations Trump Asked McGahn to Contact Rosenstein And Have Mueller Removed For "conflict of interest" Reasons... Saying "Mueller has to go"... Leading to Obstruction of Justice: Trump's Possible McGahn WH DART BOARD

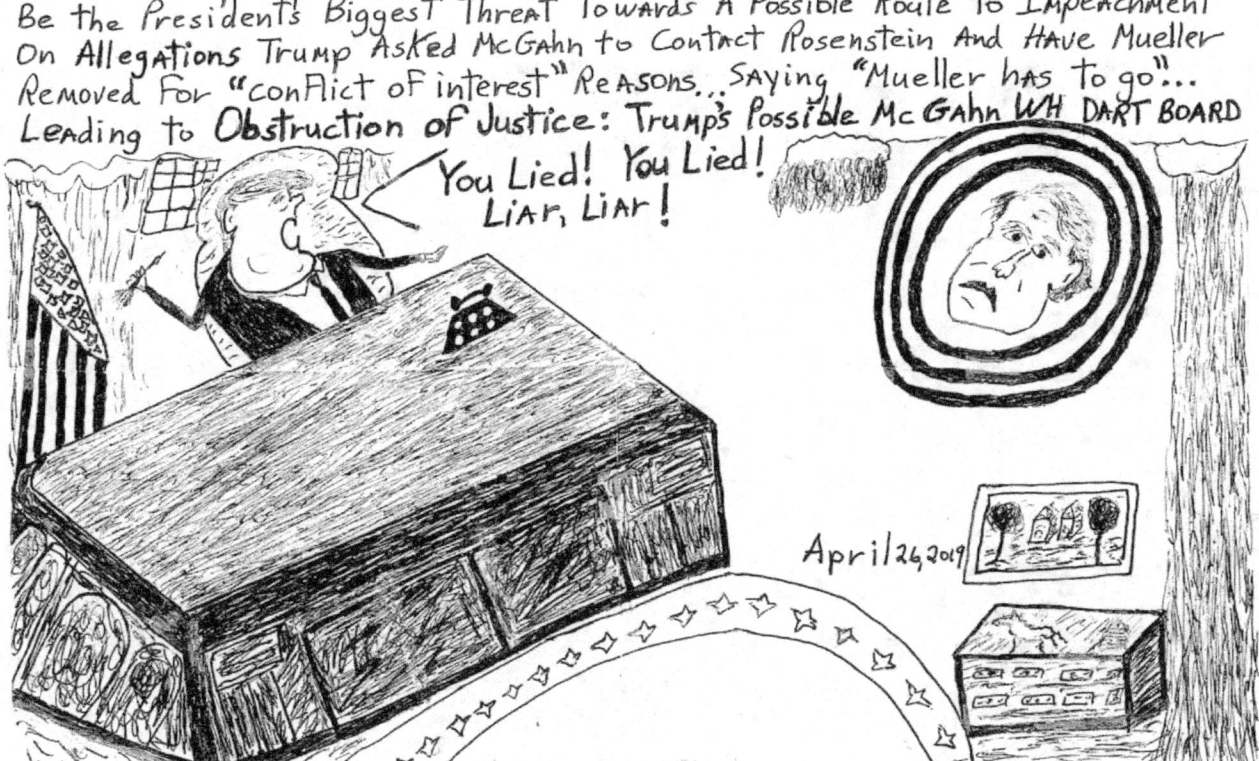

You Lied! You Lied! Liar, Liar!

April 26, 2019

Trump's Deputy Attorney General Who Oversaw Mueller Russia Probe And After FBI Director Comey Was Fired Suggested Secretly Recording Trump And Invoking the 25th Amendment to Remove Trump From Office Submits Resignation Letter... Excerpts From Rod Rosenstein's Letter, Rosenstein's Fear of Being... Tweet Targeted by Trump, And Rosenstein's Tweet Nightmare... April 30, 2019

① Excerpts... Dear Mr. President:

   Our nation is safer, our elections are more secure, And our citizens are better informed About covert foreign influence efforts.

   As I submit my resignation effective on May 11, I am grateful to you for the opportunity to serve; for the courtesy And humor you often display, And for the goals you set in your inaugural address: patriotism, unity, safety, education, And prosperity, because a nation exists to serve its citizens... Concluding: We keep the faith, we follow the rules, And we Always put America First.   Sincerely,
                    Rod J. Rosenstein

② According to Washington Post... Rosenstein in A meeting called by WH Chief of Staff John Kelly said... "I can go. I'm ready to go. I can resign. But I don't want to go out with A tweet."

Donald J. Trump ✓
@realDonaldTrump

③ Just Fired Mr. Peepers AKA Former Deputy Attorney General Rod Rosenstein.

Trump's Attorney General Barr Missing House Judiciary Hearing Sets Bill Barr Up For Below Encounter With Chairman Nadler In Pursuit of the Full Mueller Report...

May 3, 2019

Trump's Telephone Call To Putin... An Excerpt Where They Discussed As Trump Put It The "Russian Hoax". Trump Conveyed the Threat of Russian Interference in the 2020 Presidential Election Was Never Talked About. Below Joking About the "Russian Hoax"... May 3, 2019

Trump's Attorney General Barr Defends Himself Amid Calls For His Resignation From Democrats Who Accuse Him Of Misleading Congress About the Mueller's Team's Concerns Over His Description of their Findings... Answering Sen. Patrick Leahy's question... Why did you say you did NOT Know whether Mueller supported your First 4 page conclusion of insufficient evidence to say the President had obstructed justice?   May 3, 2019

① I don't Know what that refers to At All.

② OK, After receiving that letter you referred to, I spoke with the special counsel by phone. And he conveyed he thought my Findings were not inaccurate.

That letter from Mueller's team was a bit snitty, and I think it was probably written by one of his staff people.

Hon. William Barr
Attorney General
U.S. Department of Justice

③ Merriam-Webster defines "snitty" After Barr describes the Mueller letter...
To be 'snitty' is to be disagreeably ill-tempered.

④ CONCLUSION...
Given On Jan. 15, 2019 Barr said Trump's use of "Witch Hunt" is understandable.
It is conceivable Barr was referring to a "snitty" Witch Hunter!

Trump Basically Plays Patty-Cake With North Korean Leader Kim Jong Un
In Below Tweet Following Leader's Short-Range Ballistic Missile Tests And A
Possible Post Card of Leader Supervising Test Sent to Trump... The Trump
Administration Pointed Out No Long-Range Missile Tests Have Happened since 2017.
The New Missiles Tested Put the Entire Korean Peninsula Within Range ... May 4, 2019

Donald J. Trump ✓
@realDonaldTrump

Anything in this very interesting world
is possible, but I believe that Kim Jong Un
fully realizes the great economic
potential of North Korea, & will do
nothing to interfere or end it. He also
knows that I am with him & does not
want to break his promise to me.
Deal will happen!   9:42 AM - May 4, 2019

Hi President Trump!
Greeting From East
Sea. All Missile hit
bull-eye! Very Happy
You Like Missile Test!
WILL DO MORE! ALWAYS KIM

The Trump Joe Biden Nightmare that Triggered Trump's Dresden Bombing of Biden On Twitter Following Biden Getting the Endorsement of the Top Firefighters' Union   May 4, 2019

Trump's Fantastic Dream Following His Tweet Attacking Mueller Testifying to Congress... Saying Dems Want A Redo Because they Hated **NO COLLUSION** conclusion. No Redos For the Dems!
May 5, 2019

Trump Rejoices As His Senate Republicans Rally Behind Him As Senate Majority Leader Mitch McConnell Rails Against Mueller Report Proclaiming "CASE CLOSED"... Prior to Senate Issuing Subpoena For Trump's Oldest Son.   May 7, 2019

This investigation went on for two years. It's finally over. No Collusion. CASE CLOSED, CASE CLOSED.

That's my Fantastic Senate! First they pass My biggest TAX Cut in U.S. history. And now they have ended the biggest Treason Conspiracy in the history of our country!

Trump's Defiance Escalates As House Judiciary Votes to Hold Barr In Contempt For Defying Mueller Report Subpoena... As Attorney General Barr Comforts The President...
May 8, 2019
Mr. President this Executive Privilege blanket is guaranteed for the life of your presidency!
EXECTIVE BLANKET
That's Fantastic! That's a lifetime GUARANTEE!

Trump Justifies His Losses of More than $1 Billion From 1985 to 1994 In Below
Tweet... And the Ghost of President Reagan Appears To Collect Back Taxes
From Trump... Via Enforcing Reagan's Tax Reform Act of 1986... May 9, 2019

Donald J. Trump [✓] @ realDonaldTrump • May 8

Real estate developers of the 1980's
& 1990's, more than 30 years ago, were entitled
to massive write offs and depreciation which
would, if one was actively building, show losses
and tax losses in almost all cases. Much was
non monetary. Sometimes considered "tax shelter,"...
... you would get it by building, or even buying.
You always wanted to show losses for tax purposes...
Almost all real estate developers did - and often
re-negotiate with banks, it was sport. Additionally,
the very old information put out is a highly
inaccurate FAKE NEWS hit job!

① Mr. Trump my 1986 Tax Act
restricted deductions, shelters,
and loopholes. I want your tax
returns for those years!

③ I heard that Mnuchin is more
afraid of you than ghosts!

② You'll have to haunt my
Secretary of the Treasury,
Steve Mnuchin!

④ Mnuchin is a strict
Constitutionalist. He obeys
the TRUMP CONSTITUTION!

Trump Reportedly Calls Attorney General Barr to Demand Investigation of Hillary Clinton Before His Personal Attorney, Rudy Giuliani Even Leaves For Kiev, Ukraine to Have New Government there Investigate Her. Basically Seeking to Create A Kangaroo Justice Department. Given Barr Had Refused to Deny Having Been told to Investigate Anybody For Trump... Below... Exchange Between Senator Kamala Harris And Attorney General Barr At Senate Judiciary Committee Hearing Days Ago...   May 10, 2019

Attorney General Barr has the president or Anyone At the White House ever Asked or suggested that you open An investigation of. Anyone?

Can you re-re-repeat the question! I'M trying to grapple with the word suggest, I mean, there have been discussions of Matters out there that they have not Asked me to open An investigation on...

MS. HARRIS

Hon. William Barr
Attorney General
U.S. Department of Justi

Trump Basically Says He Thinks It Would Be "Appropriate" For Him & Attorney General William Barr to Talk About An Investigation Into Joe Biden Like They Could Form A Justice Partnership As Gangs Did To Sell Liquor In the 1920's During Prohibition... May 11, 2019

Trump In An Interview with <u>Politico</u>...↓

I have not at this point spoken with Attorney General Barr About An inquiry into this 2020 potential election opponent. But it certainly would be An Appropriate thing to discuss. Certainly it is A very big issue And we'll see what happens. It's not off the table...

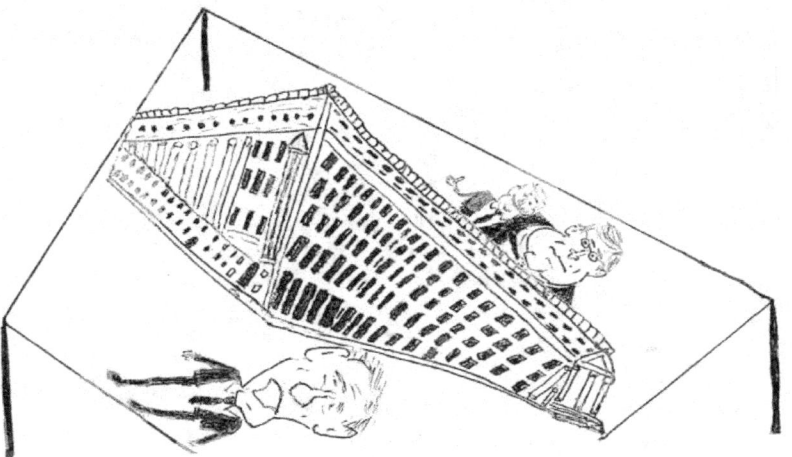

Trump Says He Did Not Order Attorney General William Barr To Launch An Investigation Into the Origins of the Russia Probe, But that He Is Proud of Barr For Doing It...
And the Historical Comparison to Robespierre, the Architect of the French Revolution's Reign of Terror. Who encouraged the execution, mostly by guillotine of more than 17,000 enemies of the Revolution From 1793-1794...
May 14, 2019
July 26, 1794
I Knew nothing about it... And it's the greatest thing! I Knew nothing about it!
I Knew nothing about All these people losing their heads!

Trump Says Democrats' Investigations Will Help Him Win In 2020 And The Ghost of Nixon Returns to the Oval Office to Offer Advice...

May 15, 2019

Trump's Pentagon Moves Additional Firepower Into the Middle East In Response to
What the Administration Says Are "Credible Threats" On U.S. Troops. The Greatest Risk
Will Come When Our Naval Ships Pass Close To Iran Through the Strait of Hormuz Below.
Where Any Individual Who Wants War Between The U.S. And Iran Could Just Attack
The Abraham Lincoln...

MAY 15, 2019

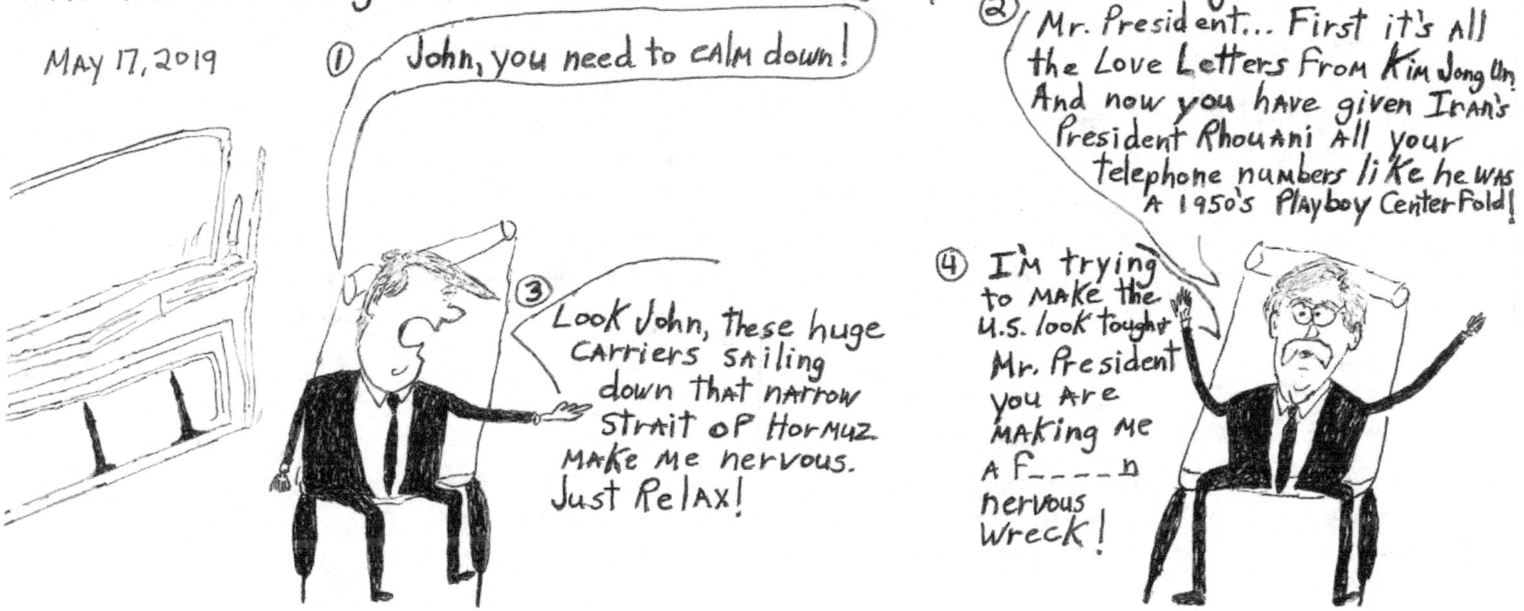

Private Citizen William Barr's Resume To Trump That Was the Foundation For His May 8, 2019 Letter to the President Requesting that he: Invoke Executive Privilege Over the Justice Department Documents Related to the Mueller Report that the House Judiciary Committee had Requested...

Legal Position On A President Obstructing Justice... It is impossible for A sitting president to obstruct justice. Because As the head of the Executive Branch, it would be As if he had obstructed himself.

Past Legal Opinions On Presidential Power... Trump Asking then -FBI Director James Comey to let go of the investigation into former national security Adviser Michael Flynn And later Firing Comey WAS Within his powers As head of the executive branch.

Miscellaneous Activities ... Attorney General to President George H.W. Bush

May 17, 2019

Trump's Attorney General William Barr says He is Trying to Determine Whether
Or Not "government officials abused their power and put their thumb on the
scale" during the early stages of the Russia probe, Trump at Realtors Meeting, and Trump Tweet...

Trump at National Assoc. of Realtors Meeting
MAY 17, 2019

① FBI Director James Comey,
Director of National Intelligence,
James Clapper, & CIA Director
John Brennan are gone!
We're draining the SWAMP!

② People have to find out
what the government
was doing during that
period...
I'm not saying that
happened but it's
something we have to
look at. MAY 17, 2019

Donald J. Trump ✓
@realDonaldTrump

③ My campaign for President was
conclusively spied on. Nothing
like this has ever happened in
American Politics. A really bad
situation. TREASON means long
jail sentences, and this was
TREASON!

6:11 AM MAY 17, 2019

④ Conclusion: Trump
Justice...

My
Fellow
Americans
the Treasonous
trio I spoke
of are going
to jail for a
long time. Justice
has been served.
SWAMP DRAINED!

Trump's Dream of a Wrestling Match With GOP Rep. Justin Amash After the Congressman Said the President "engaged in impeachable conduct."
And the President Shot Back on
Twitter... Never a Fan of @justinamash,
a total lightweight...
May 20, 2019

BYE LOSER!
What a lightweight folks!

Trump's Former Attorney, Don McGahn By Refusing To Comply With the House Judiciary Committee's Chairman, Jerry Nadler Subpoena For His Testimony Goes From Being the Monkey In The Middle to Trump's Monkey... May 20, 2019 Signaling to the President He Will Follow White House Directive NOT to Turn Over Documents Related to the Mueller Report...

Attorney General Barr Who is on the Front Lines of the President's Battles
Against Congress Says He Is Fighting For the Office of Presidency NOT Trump...
May 21, 2019

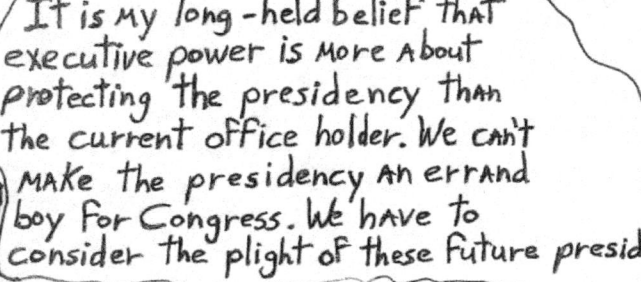

It is my long-held belief that executive power is more about protecting the presidency than the current office holder. We can't make the presidency an errand boy for Congress. We have to consider the plight of these future presidents...

Trump Walks Out on Pelosi & Schumer After 3 Minutes In Oval Office Following
Pelosi Accusing Him of A "Cover-up" Aimed At Blocking Oversight Into Russian election
Meddling Related to the Mueller Report. Amid Rising Iranian Tensions As Putin Watches
From the Kremlin While talking to North Korean Leader, Kim Jong un... May 22, 2019
A Possibility... After Trump Says NO Infrastructure Bill While
Democrats Continue to Investigate Him...

Kim, America Can't Fix its roads
And bridges. Can't wait for
their 2020 Election!

I don't do
cover-ups

Trump Gives Sweeping Powers to his Attorney General to Investigate the Investigators eg. William Barr Now Has the Power to Declassify U.S. Secrets that "Dwarf the Right" of the CIA & FBI to Protest... Basically Making William P. Barr the U.S. Reichsfuhrer of the Trump Investigation ... <u>Summary of Trump's Memorandum on Barr Review</u> May 23, 2019

Ⓘ The heads of All elements of the intelligence community shall promptly provide such Assistance and information As the Attorney General may request in connection with that review of Intelligence Activities Relating to the 2016 Presidential Campaigns.

Ⓘ The Attorney General may declassify information or intelligence that relates to the Attorney General's review.

Ⓘ <u>Trump's Conclusion...</u> The Authority in this memorandum shall terminate upon A vacancy in the office of Attorney General, unless expressly extended by the President.

Ⓘ <u>Translation of Trump's Conclusion...</u> The Authority in this memorandum shall terminate upon vacancy of my great & fantastically loyal Attorney General, unless expressly extended by this President through the Appointment of A successor equally As fantastic And loyal... Which frankly I don't think is possible...

A TRUMP FLASHBACK Given Trump Has Given His Attorney General Basically
Reichsführer Status Over American Intelligence Agencies For: In His Own Words...
Maybe the outcome of the investigation will be good, maybe not so good. MAY24,2019

Trump During Israeli Visit Speaks Out About Being Accused of Giving Information From Israel to
Russians About Terrorist groups loading Bombs into laptops to Blow up Airliners MAY 22, 2017

"Profiles In Courage"

Trump's Tweet Shortly After His Arrival In Japan After His National Security Adviser, John Bolton Said North Korea's Missile Tests Violated UN Security Council Resolutions: Followed by What Bolton Would Have Tweeted...

Donald J. Trump ✓
@realDonald Trump

John Bolton ✓
@real Donald Trump Land

North Korea fired off some small weapons, which disturbed some of my people, And others, but not me. I have confidence that Chairman Kim will keep his promise to me, & also smiled when he called Swampman Joe Biden a low IQ individual, & worse. Perhaps that's sending me a signal?

1:32 AM - May 26, 2019

Wish I was a low IQ idiot individual that could not understand any of these f____n signals!

Trump Dismisses North Korea's Missile Launches As Firing off "Small Weapons" Just Before Japanese Prime Minister Takes Trump to Sumo Wrestling Match. When Over:
May 26, 2019
Trump Presents Trophy to Champion. Shinzo Abe's Thoughts Behind Smile...
Now good time me order siren for North Korea Missile Drill!

Trump Appears to be Backing Down From Bolton's U.S. Carrier Move On Iran: Saying...
"Sometimes He Has to Control Security Adviser John Bolton." Whose Push For Confrontation
With Tehran Was Ignored More Than A Decade Ago by President George W. Bush...

May 17, 2019

① John, you need to CALM down!

② Mr. President... First it's All the Love Letters From Kim Jong Un, And now you have given Iran's President Rhouani All your telephone numbers like he was a 1950's Playboy Centerfold!

③ Look John, these huge carriers sailing down that narrow Strait of Hormuz Make me nervous. Just Relax!

④ I'm trying to make the U.S. look tough Mr. President you are making me a F____n nervous wreck!

Attorney General Barr Who is on the Front Lines of the President's Battles Against Congress Says He Is Fighting For the Office of Presidency NOT Trump...
May 21, 2019

It is my long-held belief that executive power is more about protecting the presidency than the current office holder. We can't make the presidency an errand boy for Congress. We have to consider the plight of these future presidents...

Trump Calls Himself An "Extremely Stable Genius" At Wild Press Conference And Asks Staff to Vouch For His Calm Stability: What Trump Might Have Forgot Mentioning to Support His Genius...

May 23, 2019

A TRUMP FLASHBACK Given Trump Has Given His Attorney General Basically Reichsfuhrer Status Over American Intelligence Agencies For: In His Own Words... Maybe the outcome of the investigation will be good, maybe not so good. MAY24,2019

Trump During Israeli Visit Speaks Out About Being Accused of Giving Information From Israel to Russians About Terrorist groups loading Bombs into laptops to Blow Up Airliners MAY 22,2017

Just, so you understand, And, I never mentioned the word or the name Israel!

Our Intelligence sharing is terrific. Tonight we Are sharing delicious Matzo ball soup And My wife's secret Jewish Kreplach recipes

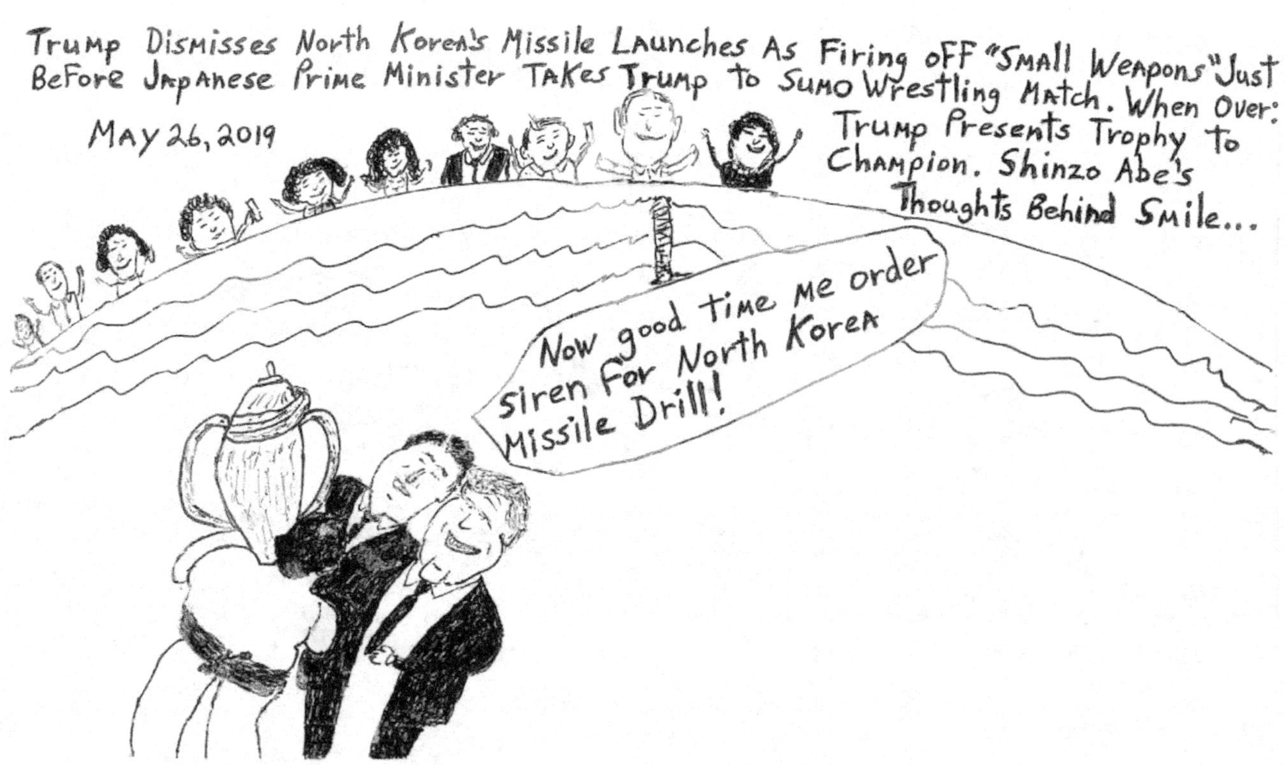

"Profiles In Courage"

Trump's Tweet Shortly After His Arrival In Japan After His National Security Adviser, John Bolton Said North Korea's Missile Tests Violated UN Security Council Resolutions: Followed by What Bolton Would Have Tweeted...

 Donald J. Trump ✓
@ realDonald Trump

North Korea fired off some small weapons, which disturbed some of my people, and others, but not me. I have confidence that Chairman Kim will keep his promise to me, & also smiled when he called SWAMPMAN Joe Biden a low IQ individual, & worse. Perhaps that's sending me a signal?

1:32 AM - May 26, 2019

John Bolton ✓
@ real Donald Trump Land

Wish I was a low IQ idiot individual that could not understand any of these f____n signals!

A TALE OF TWO JUSTICE DEPARTMENTS... Mueller vs. Barr   FACT vs Fairy Tale

MAY 29, 2019

MAY 29, 2019

< Good Morning... If we had had confidence the President did **not** commit a crime we would have said so. We did not however make a determination as to whether the President committed a crime. There was insufficent evidence to charge a broader conspiracy. Under long standing department policy a president can not be charged with a crime while in office. Therefore, charging the president with a crime was **not** an option. <u>Bottom Line...</u> I'm tired and I want to just PLAY BINGO NOW!

March 24, 2019

< Good Morning... The evidence developed by the special counsel is **not** sufficent to establish that the president committed an obstruction of justice offense. The Russian operatives who perpetrated these **schemes** did not have the cooperation of the Trump campaign or President Trump. We specifically asked the Special Prosecutor if the office of Legal Counsel's opinion of **not** charging a sitting President influenced him... He said **NO**. <u>Bottom Line</u>... Walt Disney could **not** create a better FAIRY TALE...

Trump Says the Navy Official Who Directed Obscuring USS John S. McCain In Japan Was "Well-Meaning" Going to Great Lengths to Shield President From Seeing the Ship...

Trump's Tweet "I had nothing to do with Russia helping me to get elected"
Followed by Trump telling Reporters that Russia Didn't help him get elected in 2016 And Putin...

① Donald J. Trump ✓ @ realDonaldTrump

Russia, Russia, Russia! That's all
you heard at the beginning of
this Witch Hunt Hoax... And now Russia
has disappeared because I had nothing
to do with Russia helping me to get
elected. It was a crime that didn't
exist. So now the Dems and their partner,
the Fake News Media,......

7:57 AM May 30, 2019

② Russia did not help me get
elected... You know who got me
elected, You know who got me
elected, I got me elected! Russia
didn't help me at all. Russia, if
Anything helped the other side...

Russian President Vladimir Putin July 16, 2018 At A News Conference During Trump-Putin
Summit in Helsinki...
Asked if he wanted
President Donald Trump
to win the 2016
election...

③ Yes, I did. Yes, I did. Because he talked
About bringing the U.S. - Russia
relationship back to normal.

Trump Threatens Mexico With Tariffs To Stop Illegal Migrants From Central-America Coming Up Into the U.S. Without Specifically Defining His Goal... Working Out the Details with Senior Advisor For Policy Stephen Miller... ↓

Donald J. Trump ✓ @ real Donald Trump

On June 10th, the United States will impose A 5% Tariff on All goods coming into our Country From Mexico, until such time As illegal Migrants coming through Mexico, And into our Country, STOP. The Tariff will gradually increase until the Illegal Immigration problem is remedied...

Donald J. Trump ✓ @ real Donald Trump

.... At which time the Tariffs will be removed. Details From the White House to Follow.

7:30 PM - May 30, 2019

Mr. President, like you said... We want the best And brightest! No Salvation Army CARAVANS. Therefore, we will only Accept Migrants in well-dressed Attire (preferably Louis Vuitton) who Are chauffeured with Bentley's or Rolls Royces.

Trump In Oval Office Watching MSNBC's, The 11th Hour When Host Brian Williams Plays the Voicemail of then Trump's Personal Attorney, John Dowd to Michael Flynn's Attorney On the Eve of Flynn's Plea Deal, Asking Rob Kelner For A "heads up"...

May 31, 2019

< Here's the November of 2017 voicemail of the President's Attorney, John Dowd, Folks...

① Hey, Rob, uhm, this is John Again. Look, I'd like A heads up About Any information that... implicates the President, then we've got A national security issue, we got to - we got to deal with, not only For the President, but For the country. So... uh... you Know, then - then, you know, we need some Kind of heads up. Um, just For the sake of protecting All our interests, if we can, without you having to give up Any... confidential information.

② My Ass lawyer Dowd MAKes Low IQ Joe Biden look like Albert Einstein! MAKing A f_____ voice mail recording! A f_____ RECORDING!

Trump's Acting Chief of Staff Mick Mulvaney Defends White House Request To Hide USS John S. McCain During President's Visit to Japan...On Meet The Press...   June 2, 2019

① Do you think the request from the White House to hide the USS John S. McCain during the President's trip to Japan was reasonable?

③ A better question... I better not ask...

If the destroyer U.S.S. John S. McCain was the closest torpedo ship to a naval conflict with China in the South China Sea, would it be reasonable to consider the President's feelings in Naval Strategy?

MEET THE PRESS

② The fact that some 23 or 24 year old person on the advance team went to that sight and said, oh my goodness, here's the John McCain, we all know how the president feels about the former senator, maybe that's not the best backdrop, can somebody look into moving it. That's not an unreasonable thing... If you're going to a staff meeting and say, Look, Chuck is fighting with so-and-so. Let's not sit them together, is that a firable offense at NBC?

Trump's Tweet Hours Before Landing In London,
Joining The Royals, & Possible Getting Back At London's Mayor.....

Donald J. Trump ✓ @realDonaldTrump
@Sadiq Khan, who by All Accounts
      has done a terrible job As Mayor
of London, has been foolishly "nasty" to
the visiting President of the United States,
by far the most important Ally of the
United Kingdom. He is a stone loser
who should focus on crime in London,
not me.....   June 3, 2019

Maybe I Can Do A DEAL with
this Queen!
I use my Tariff Power to help the
next Prime Minister get a good
Brexit Agreement in exchange For
her naming me, Donald J. Trump,
Duke of London - That'll fix that
LOSER MAYOR.....

House Judiciary Chairman Jerry Nadler Refuses the Justice Department's Offer to Reopen Negotiations on Committee's Subpoena for the Full Mueller Report... Justice Wanted the Judiciary Committee to Drop their Vote in Favor of Barr Charged with Contempt... That Was Headed to the Full House For A Vote...

June 4, 2019

② The President As head of the Executive branch can not obstruct justice. Therefore, the President can not be charged with obstructing himself. And the Attorney General is in Contempt of NOTHING!

Can you substitute contempt with Another legal term?

① Tell Nadler I'm still trying to grapple with the word contempt...

③ Sure! We can charge you with being A Bona Fide Asshole!

Senate Republicans Gently Push Back On Trump's Threatened Tariffs On Mexico... With A Threat to Override President's Veto... Below Senators Mitch McConnell & Chuck Grassley Try Their Luck With A TRUMP STATUE...

June 5, 2019

Trump's Tale of Two Trips to Normandy for D-Day Commemoration: First Stop, the Normandy American Cemetery Where He Waged His War Against Nancy Pelosi And Robert Mueller... Then Having Made His Cemetery Commemoration, It Was presidential speech time...

June 6, 2019

That Robert Mueller Made such a Fool out of himself. He had to write a letter to straighten out his False testimony. And Nancy Pelosi, I call her Nervous Nancy. She is a nasty, vindictive, and horrible person. She is a disaster, a disaster!

You are among the very greatest Americans - who will ever live. You are the glory of our republic, and we thank you from the bottom of our hearts.

Trump's Private Thoughts On Air Force One to the U.S. Navy Calling the Incident of A Russian Destroyer Nearly Colliding With An American Guided-Missile Cruiser As "Unsafe And Unprofessional". Given the Russian Pacific Fleet Blamed the U.S. For the Close Call. Given Trump Has Not Publicly Responded. And given Trump's Past Statements Basically Believing Putin's Denials... June 7, 2019

The Russians could have mistaken this American guided-missile cruiser For A certain U.S. Destroyer named After A Senator the Fake-News Media has driven them to believe I can't even look At. I know my ships. And Cruisers And Destroyers really look very much alike.
Another incident caused by the FAKE-NEWS MEDIA!

Trump's Tweet On the Suspension of Tariff Threats Against Mexico, With Comments From Trump Senior Counselor, Kelly Anne Conway, Concluding With A Hypothetical Question The Late Walter Cronkite Would Have Asked ...

Donald J. Trump @ realDonaldTrump
We have Fully signed and documented
Another very important part of the
Immigration and Security deal with Mexico,
one that the U.S. has been Asking About
getting For many years. It will be revealed
in the not too distant Future, and will need
A vote by Mexico's Legislative body!..
.... We do not Anticipate a problem with
the vote but, if For Any reason the Approval
is not Forthcoming, Tariffs will be reinstated!
6:31 AM - June 10, 2019

Kelly Anne Conway, Senior Trump
Counselor On Fox News...

Mexico took the
President's tariFF
threat very seriously,
This is important
For both countries-
We now have Mexico
doing More than
Democrats to secure our
SOUTHERN BORDER!

I can't
talk about
All the
details yet.
I am not
here to talk
About the
President's Tweets
this Morning.

What is
the secret
deal that
Mexico Knows
nothing About?!

Trump At White House South Lawn On Impeachment And Nixon: On the same day that Former President Nixon's White House Counsel, John Dean Testified About the Parallels Between Trump And Richard M. Nixon

June 11, 2019

① "You can't impeach somebody when there's never been a thing done wrong. When you look at past impeachments, whether it was President Clinton, or I guess President Nixon, never got there - he left. I don't leave. Big Difference..."

Trump Says He Would Welcome Any Foreign Country's Information to Basically Help Him Win In 2020 And Would Take It Again From Russia IF They Offered Dirt On An Opponent... Sounding A Repeat Performance of July 27, 2016 When Trump Called On Russia to Find presidential Democratic nominee Hillary Clinton's Missing eMails... Here Now Putin's June 13, 2019 Response...

Comrade Stalin 2020 is going to be EASIER than even 2016 WAS. All we have to do is secure Trump's base And split up Biden's support. And get Biden to Appear More And More to the Liberal Left. Driving Folks into Camp Trump. I would say with everybody talking About landing the plane... America is on Automatic Pilot. All we have to do is rev up their engines... Like A TUNE-UP!

Trump's Fantastic Dream of Having A Warm & Loving Relationship With Iran's Supreme Leader. Following: Trump Receiving A Reply From Japanese Prime Minister Shinzo Abe that the Supreme Leader Regarded His Note As "Not Worthy" of Reply, Iran's Attack on Oil Tankers in the Gulf Waters, And Fox News Interview... June 13, 2019

PRESIDENT TRUMP LIVE ON FOX & FRIENDS

On Iranian Attack on oil Tankers in Gulf Waters... They did it. But there is no More screaming of "Death to America" like when Barack Obama was U.S. president. On North Korea... No More Nuke Tests And Long Range Missiles... Just letting Short Range!

Trump In An ABC News Interview Says "I never suggested Firing Mueller" Despite His Former WH Counsel John McGahn's Testimony that Trump Said "Mueller has to go-call Me when it's done." Trump Claims... McGahn "MAY have been confused" Because...
June 14, 2019

Trump's Next Move On Justice Department After It Releases Legal Opinion Backing
Treasury Secretary Steven Mnuchin's Refusal to Release President's Tax Returns to
Congress...
June 14, 2019

This will be the Justice Wing of the White House!

Pollster Officials Possibly Leaked Polls Showing Trump Losing Because of the President's Denial of their Existence... Leads to the Result of the President Changing the Messenger by Firing Three Longtime Pollsters. Below... the FOX NEWS POLL ↓ And PLAN B For the Pollster Officials...

① 2020 VOTE FOR PRESIDENT IF VOTING NOW

DEMOCRATIC CANDIDATE		DONALD TRUMP
JOE BIDEN	49%	39%
BERNIE SANDERS	49%	40%
ELIZABETH WARREN	43%	41%
KAMALA HARRIS	42%	41%
PETE BUTTIGIEG	41%	40%

② PLAN B POLL RELEASE OF

JOE THE PLUMBER v. DONALD TRUMP June 18, 2019

JOE THE PLUMBER
48%

DONALD TRUMP
38%

A Private Possible Meeting Between Trump & His Acting Chief of Staff Mick Mulvaney Following Trump Kicking Mulvaney Out of the Oval Office for Coughing During A Stephanopoulos ABC Interview

June 18, 2019

Trump Launches His Campaign For Re-Election At Orlando Rally... And Putin Responds to.... "Nobody's been tougher on Russia than Donald Trump" June 18, 2019

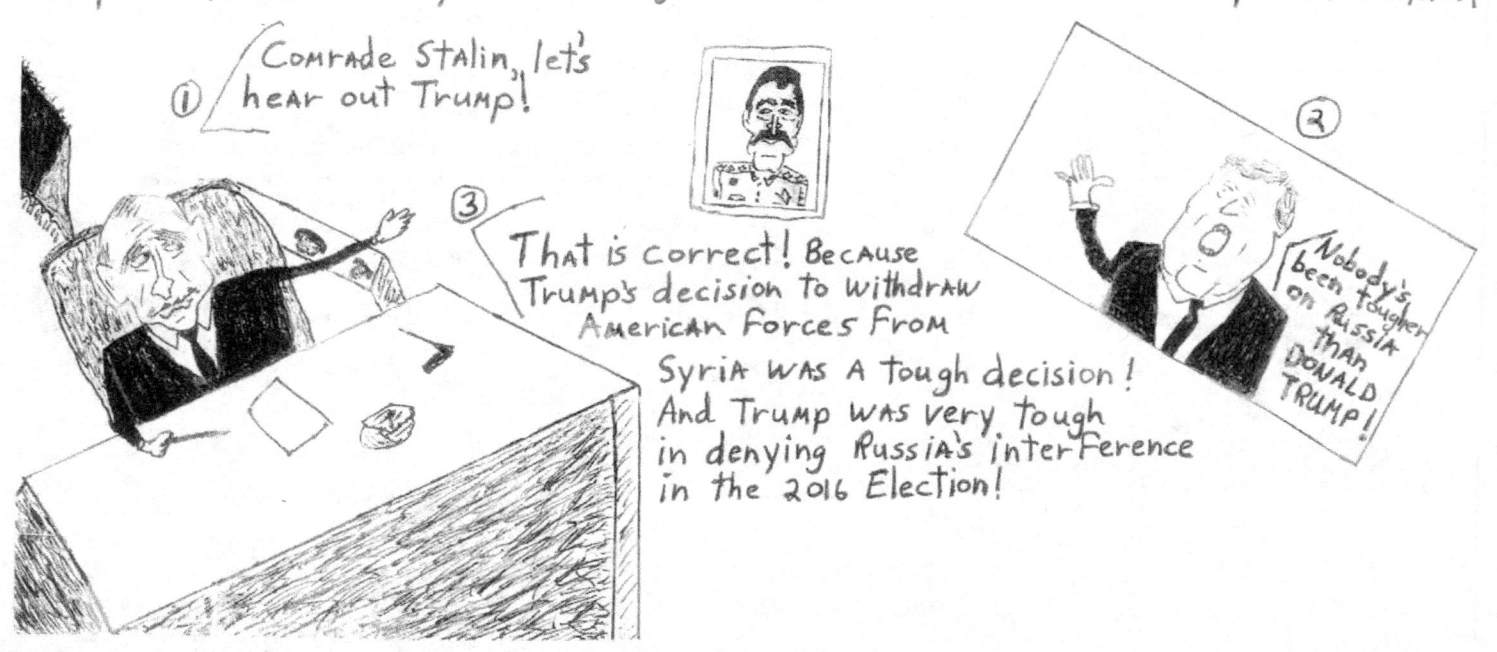

Trump's National Security Advisor + Former Fox News Contributor, John Bolton June 22, 2019
Following Trump's Last-Minute Reversal on Striking Iran Visits Psychiatrist For Counseling...

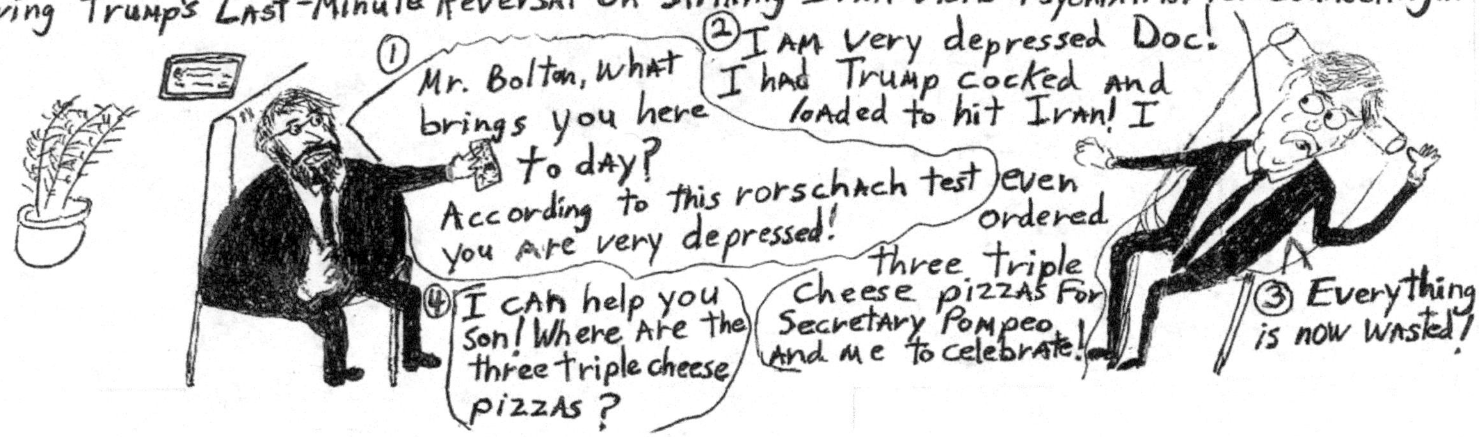

Trump On Photo Of Drowned Father And Daughter Trying to Swim Across the Rio Grande ... Basically Blames the Democrats For Wanting Open Borders. "Open Borders Mean Crime And Open Borders Mean People Drowning In the River!" "And it's A Very dangerous thing"!

June 26, 2019

TRUMP DECODED... What He Did Not Say...

I hate it! And I know it could stop immediately if the Democrats change the law. And then that Father probably who was this wonderful guy with his daughter. But we don't know For sure. He might have been A terrorist killer!

Trump, With A Smiling Grin, Tells Putin: "Don't Meddle in the Election"
Basically Giving Putin A Green Light To Have Some Thoughts For 2020...
June 28, 2019

Putin Invites Trump to 75th Annual WWII Victory Parade in Red Square At Their G-20 Meeting In Osaka, Japan: Following Trump's Warm Response to the Invitation, A Kremlin Spokesman Said the pair went on to Discuss "each Country's Losses" During the War... Excerpt From Trump News Conference On Russian Losses...

June 29, 2019

President Putin told Me Russian losses were 25 Million. But some people told Me it WAS AS high AS 50 Million!

It WAS 50 Million!

It WAS 50 Million!

PRESIDENT OF The United...

Trump's Nightmare After Shaking Hands with North Korean Leader Kim Jong Un And Crossing Into North Korea that Led to A Commitment Between the Two Nations to Restart Nuclear Talks. Given Kim Sung-han, A former South Korean Vice-Minister of Foreign Affairs said... "If Kim loses Again, I think that Will be somewhat Fatal to his regime security." And the Trump Administration has touted the Absence of long-range Missile testing As evidence its Approach with North Korea is Working.....

June 30, 2019

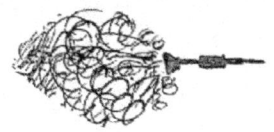

At least it shows he's really thinking of me. And not just reading my tweets!

Trump Meets With China President Xi Jinping Allowing U.S Sales to Chinese Tech Giant Huawei, Halting Additional Tariffs On Chinese Goods And Agreeing to Restart Trade Talks... Basically Trump is Suddenly Fine With Chinese Telecom Huawei After He Called it A "National-Security Threat"...

Back in May, the Trump Administration Had Placed Huawei On A Trade Blacklist Following the Unsealing Of A Justice Department Indictment that Said the Company Had Conspired to Provide Forbidden Financial Services to Iran. And Concluded it Was Engaged in Activities Hostile to U.S Interests...

June 30, 2019

Trump Justifies His Losses of More than $1 Billion From 1985 to 1994 In Below
Tweet... And the Ghost of President Reagan Appears To Collect Back Taxes
From Trump... Via Enforcing Reagan's Tax Reform Act of 1986...   May 9, 2019

Donald J. Trump ✔ @ real Donald Trump • May 8

Real estate developers of the 1980's
+ 1990's, more than 30 years ago, were entitled
to massive write offs and depreciation which
would, if one was actively building, show losses
and tax losses in almost all cases. Much was
non monetary. Sometimes considered "tax shelter"...
... you would get it by building, or even buying.
You always wanted to show losses for tax purposes...
Almost all real estate developers did - and often
re-negotiate with banks, it was sport. Additionally,
the very old information put out is a highly
inaccurate FAKE News hit job!

① Mr. Trump My 1986 Tax Act
restricted deductions, shelters,
and loopholes. I want your tax
returns for those years!

③ I heard that Mnuchin is more
afraid of you than ghosts!

② You'll have to haunt my
Secretary of the Treasury,
Steve Mnuchin!

④ Mnuchin is a strict
Constitutionalist. He obeys
the TRUMP CONSTITUTION!

Trump's Fantastic Dream of Having A Warm & Loving Relationship With Iran's Supreme Leader. Following: Trump Receiving A Reply From Japanese Prime Minister Shinzo Abe that the Supreme Leader Regarded His Note As "Not Worthy" of Reply, Iran's Attack on Oil Tankers in the Gulf Waters, And Fox News Interview... June 13, 2019

PRESIDENT TRUMP LIVE ON FOX & FRIENDS

On Iranian Attack on oil tankers in Gulf Waters... They did it. But there is no more screaming of "Death to America" like when Barack Obama was U.S. president On North Korea... No More Nuke Tests And Long Range Missiles... Just letting Short Range!